School-Based Prevention Programs for Children and Adolescents

Joseph A. Durlak

Volume 34
Developmental Clinical Psychology and Psychiatry

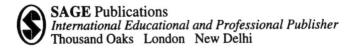

SAGE Publications
International Educational and Professional Publisher
Thousand Oaks   London   New Delhi

For information address:

 SAGE Publications, Inc.
2455 Teller Road
Thousand Oaks, California 91320
Email: order@sagepub.com

SAGE Publications Ltd.
6 Bonhill Street
London EC2A 4PU
United Kingdom

SAGE Publications India Pvt. Ltd.
M-32 Market
Greater Kailash I
New Delhi 110 048 India

Printed in the United States of America

Library of Congress Cataloging-in-Publication Data

Durlak, Joseph A.
    School-based prevention programs for children and adolescents/
Joseph A. Durlak.
        p. cm.—(Development clinical psychology and psychiatry:
v. 34)
    Includes bibliographical references and index.
    ISBN 0-8039-5631-2 (cloth: alk. paper).—ISBN 0-8039-5632-0
(pbk: alk. paper)
    1. Students—Mental health services. 2. Youth psychopathology.
3. Adjustment (Psychology) 4. Behavior modification. I. Title.
II. Series.
LB3430.5D87   1995
373.14'6—dc20   95-12680

This book is printed on acid-free paper.

95 96 97 98 99 10 9 8 7 6 5 4 3 2 1

Sage Production Editor: Diane S. Foster

School-Based Prevention Programs for Children and Adolescents

Developmental Clinical Psychology and Psychiatry Series

Series Editor: Alan E. Kazdin, Yale University

Recent volumes in this series . . .

CONTENTS

SERIES EDITOR'S INTRODUCTION

Interest in child development and adjustment is by no means new. Yet only recently has the study of children benefited from advances in both clinical and scientific research. Advances in the social and biological sciences, the emergence of disciplines and subdisciplines that focus exclusively on childhood and adolescence, and greater appreciation of the impact of such influences as the family, peers, and school have helped accelerate research on developmental psychopathology. Apart from interest in the study of child development and adjustment for its own sake, the need to address clinical problems of adulthood naturally draws one to investigate precursors in childhood and adolescence.

Within a relatively brief period, the study of psychopathology among children and adolescents has proliferated considerably. Several different professional journals, annual book series, and handbooks devoted entirely to the study of children and adolescents and their adjustment document the proliferation of work in the field. Nevertheless, there is a paucity of resource material that presents information in an authoritative, systematic, and disseminable fashion. There is a need within the field to convey the latest developments and to represent different disciplines, approaches to, and conceptual views on the topics of childhood and adolescent adjustment and maladjustment.

The Sage Series on **Developmental Clinical Psychology and Psychiatry** is uniquely designed to serve several needs of the field. The Series encompasses individual monographs prepared by experts in the fields of clinical child psychology, child psychiatry, child development, and related disciplines. The primary focus is on developmental psychopathology, which refers broadly here to the diagnosis, assessment, treatment, and prevention of problems that arise in the period from infancy through adolescence. A working assumption of the Series is that the understanding, identification, and treatment of problems of youth must draw on multiple disciplines and on diverse views within given disciplines.

The task for individual contributors is to present the latest theory and research on various topics, including specific types of dysfunction, diagnostic and treatment approaches, and special problem areas that affect adjustment. Core topics within clinical work are addressed by the Series. Authors are asked to bridge potential theory, research, and clinical practice, and to outline the current status and future directions of research in their topic areas. The goals of the Series and the tasks presented to individual contributors are demanding. We have been extremely fortunate in recruiting leaders in their fields who have been able to translate their recognized scholarship and expertise into highly readable works on contemporary topics.

The present book, which focuses on the prevention of emotional and behavioral problems in children and adolescents, nicely illustrates the thrust, authoritativeness, and importance of the works in the Series. Prevention is of course of enormous significance. The range of mental health problems, the number of youths who experience them, the difficulties in life to which young individuals are subjected, and of course the problems involved in treating even a fraction of those in need, heighten the significance of early intervention. In the present book, Dr. Joseph A. Durlak examines school-based prevention. He discusses the advances that have been made in several areas of interest, including substance use, teen pregnancy, other health-related issues, and academic problems. The book moves from basic concepts of prevention through theory, methods, and applications. Critical topics, including characteristics of effective interventions, guidelines for research on and implementation of interventions, and the range of factors related to the dissemination of effective interventions, are presented systematically. Dr. Durlak provides a balanced account of accomplishments and limitations as well as several constructive guidelines and suggestions for the acceleration of advances in research and applications. This volume is authoritative, evenhanded, and written with remarkable clarity.

—*ALAN E. KAZDIN, PH.D.*

PREFACE

Schools are a natural environment for prevention programs because most children attend schools, and through them an infrastructure exists for reaching large numbers of children during their formative years. It may surprise the reader to learn how many prevention programs exist in schools. Each year, millions of schoolchildren are exposed to curricula that have a preventive thrust. These include sex and AIDS education, health education, substance abuse programs, academic interventions, and various efforts to promote personal and social growth. Unfortunately, the overwhelming majority of these programs have not been evaluated in any systematic fashion, and in the few cases where highly popular programs have been examined, the resulting data do not inspire much confidence in their effectiveness.

On the one hand, the fact that the practice of prevention in schools has far exceeded the science of prevention is discouraging. It is unsettling to learn that children are exposed to many interventions the results of which are unknown. Viewed from another perspective, however, this situation presents an opportunity. For various reasons, schools are willing to offer prevention-oriented programs. Research evidence is now accumulating that indicates some types of prevention efforts are successful, and we are beginning to learn some of the factors that increase or decrease positive outcomes. Therefore, we need to begin to describe which school-based prevention programs achieve the best outcomes and to discuss the factors or circumstances that contribute to this success. These are the goals of this book.

In the chapters that follow, I review the science of school-based prevention by evaluating the impact of empirically evaluated programs. Many studies have examined how programs may change knowledge and attitudes, but this book concentrates on the behavioral impact of prevention. By the end of 1994, 586 published outcome studies had appeared on this topic. The focus here is on how interventions have improved the behavioral, social, or academic adjustment of program participants, apart from any changes that have occurred in information or beliefs. Programs are divided according to their prevention goals, and the procedures and outcomes of representative interventions in each area are presented. The most promising programs and strategies are highlighted, and unresolved issues are discussed. Because it presents discussion about the prevention of several different types of problems, this book should be useful for students, faculty, and practitioners in the fields of mental health, education, public health, health psychology, applied developmental psychology, and community psychology. My hope is to stimulate further multidisciplinary work in school-based prevention, which appears to have considerable promise for improving the lives of children and adolescents.

I wish to acknowledge specifically the grant support provided by the William T. Grant Foundation of New York, which funded my work on the primary and secondary prevention of behavioral and social problems in children and adolescents (Grant No. 92147592). This work served as a basis for much of the material in Chapter 2. I also wish to thank several students who have worked with me over the past several years. In alphabetical order, they are Jill Carmody, Kelly Cotten, Kelly Johnson, Claudia Lampman, and Julie Oxenberg. In particular, I want to thank Anne Wells for her continued interest in and support of my work. I am also grateful to my colleagues at Loyola University, Fred Bryant and Steve Brown, who shared their expertise regarding meta-analysis with me. A special thanks goes to Alan Kazdin, who paid me the compliment of asking me to write this book. Finally, I want to thank my wife, Chris. She was kind enough to read through and edit early revisions of the manuscript, and she provided me with the emotional support I needed to finish my writing.

1

BASIC CONCEPTS AND APPROACHES

THE NEED FOR PREVENTION

There are several rationales for prevention, but a primary one is that our current mental health system is not reaching most children and adolescents who need help. Although improvements in therapeutic services can be made, it is unlikely that there will ever be sufficient resources within the mental health field to satisfy the need and demand for services.

For example, up to 30% of children display some form of behavioral or social maladjustment at some time during their school careers (Glidewell & Swallow, 1969). Problems are not serious or chronic for about half of these children, although their difficulties may affect their academic and social development. Between 10% and 12% of children experience moderately serious clinical problems, and between 1% and 3% have very serious problems. At the same time, estimates indicate that at best only between 10% and 30% of children with clinical-level dysfunction ever receive any mental health care (Kazdin, 1990). Such figures have led Gullotta (1994) to suggest that if prevention were found effective for only 20% of those who would otherwise develop problems, as many children would be helped as are currently being served through traditional treatment channels. In other words, large-scale prevention programs could at least double the number of children who receive needed attention. Moreover, prevention has the potential to reduce the personal, social, and economic toll that accompanies maladjustment.

The above figures referring to psychopathology do not include all the difficulties experienced by youth. Dryfoos (1990) has examined the literature in four additional areas: delinquent acts, unprotected sexual intercourse, poor academic achievement, and drug use. She estimates that

1

only half of all 10- to 17-year-olds are in a low-risk category (i.e., their risk for serious negative outcomes is minimal); however, 25% are at moderate risk, 15% are at high risk, and the remaining 10% are at very high risk. Although current information cannot pinpoint exactly what specific consequences accrue to youth in various risk categories, the notion that up to one half of our nation's young people are at risk for later adjustment problems of some form is a sobering thought.

Some contend that the current mental health system is so strained that it does not make sense to expend part of our critical resources on prevention, particularly primary prevention that involves currently normal children (Lamb & Zusman, 1979). Actually, from a public health perspective, some simple arithmetic suggests there is as great a need for primary prevention as for other forms of intervention. For instance, based on various epidemiological data, Clarizio (1979) offers the reasonable estimates that approximately 30% of clinically dysfunctional children will also have serious adjustment problems as adults, and about 8% of well-adjusted children will have similar negative outcomes in adulthood.

Currently, there are more than 47 million children in elementary and secondary schools in the United States; approximately 15% of them have clinical-level problems (Population A = 7,050,000), whereas 85% have only mild problems that will disappear over time or are otherwise well-adjusted (Population B = 39,950,000). Over time, there will be 2,115,000 disturbed adults coming from Population A (reflecting a 30% continuance rate), but there will be 3,196,000 coming from Population B (an 8% continuance rate). In other words, compared with the population of clinically distressed children, the population of normal children will contribute about 50% more cases to the population of maladjusted adults. Therefore, it does make sense to offer prevention services to children.

WHAT IS PREVENTION?

Prevention is a multidisciplinary science that draws upon basic and applied research conducted in many fields, such as public health, epidemiology, education, medicine, and community developmental and clinical psychology. Several different schemata and concepts have been proposed to define prevention and to distinguish its different manifestations. Historically, three major types of prevention have been considered in reference to when problems develop. *Primary prevention* is intervention with normal populations to preclude the occurrence of problems.

Secondary prevention involves intervention during the early development of difficulties, before they become full-blown disorders. The aim of *tertiary prevention* is to reduce the prevalence of established disorders or problems. Because tertiary prevention has often been confused with clinical treatment or rehabilitation, the Institute of Medicine (1994) recommends that only interventions offered before the onset of full-blown disorders be considered as prevention. I adopt this approach in this book and discuss only primary and secondary prevention, which I describe further below.

CONCEPTUAL APPROACHES TO PRIMARY PREVENTION

Primary prevention includes six major approaches that can be distinguished according to the level of intervention and the method used to target populations. Figure 1.1 depicts these distinctions and captures the views of several preventionists (Buckner, Trickett, & Corse, 1985; Cowen, 1986; Jason & Bogat, 1983; Price, 1986). In terms of the level of intervention, programs can be divided according to whether they focus on the person or the environment. Programs falling into the former category attempt to work directly with children to prevent specific problems or to use a skill-building or competency-building approach to teach children important behaviors or skills that will directly enhance their functioning. These interventions are often called *mental health promotion* or simply *health promotion* interventions, although the term *health promotion* can pertain to environmental programs as well.

Health promotion interventions assume that enhanced functioning resulting from skills acquisition will ultimately be preventive for any number of reasons; for example, individuals will be better able to deal with stress, will be more adept in social situations, will have greater self-confidence, or will be interpersonally more flexible and adaptable.

In contrast to person-centered interventions, environment-focused programs attempt to influence individuals indirectly, through environmental manipulations. Two basic principles behind environmental interventions (sometimes also called ecological interventions) are that there are many social and organizational influences upon behavior, and behavior cannot be considered apart from its ecological context. Environment-oriented interventions take many forms: The environment or part of it may be modified, a new environment may be created, or individuals may be

Focus of Intervention

	Person	Environment
Universal Intervention		
High-Risk Groups		
Those Undergoing Transitions		

Selection of Target Groups

Figure 1.1. Conceptual Overview of Approaches to Primary Prevention

shifted into more positive environmental situations, where, for example, they can experience less stress and more support. Environmental programs often stress the importance of studying environmental-individual interactions, because it is assumed that environments affect individuals differently. Those in one group may function best in a given type of environment, whereas those in another group may do best in another setting. Frequently, it is the child's psychosocial environment, rather than the physical environment, that is modified in such interventions, through work with parents, teachers, or peers, because these individuals play such important roles in children's lives.

The second dimension of primary prevention programs (i.e., the rows in Figure 1.1) consists of the major ways in which populations are selected or targeted for preventive work. First, in a universal or global strategy, available populations are selected. These groups are not considered to be maladjusted in any major respect or to be at risk for any particular problem. Programs for all first-grade children or all middle school children, for example, would fall into this category. In a second strategy, groups considered to be at risk for eventual problems but not yet dysfunctional are targeted for intervention. Children of alcoholics would be candidates for this type of intervention because such children are more likely than children of nonalcoholic parents to experience various adjustment problems.

The final strategy for selecting target groups is to focus on those about to experience important life transitions, developmental tasks, or stressful life events. The assumption behind this approach, called a transitions or milestone approach, is that certain events or transitions can produce negative outcomes if they are not successfully negotiated or effectively mastered by those about to experience them. Children about to enter or change schools or children with separating or divorcing parents would be suitable candidates for intervention in this approach to primary prevention.

The approaches depicted in Figure 1.1 are neither mutually exclusive nor antagonistic. Some programs fit into more than one category, and approaches are often combined in environmental programs. For example, in many early childhood interventions, children participate in day school or preschool programs designed to promote their social and cognitive development. Nevertheless, many of these programs concurrently seek to modify the children's home environments, because it is believed the long-term impact of intervention depends on the extent to which changes occur at the family level. Therefore, the major distinction between person- and environment-focused programs concerns whether or not some environmental change is being attempted. In summary, primary prevention can be defined as a collection of strategies that attempt to prevent problems from developing in currently normal populations by changing the environment, by changing individuals, or by doing both, including attempts at mental health promotion.

SECONDARY PREVENTION

Secondary prevention involves prompt intervention for subclinical-level problems. In contrast to primary prevention, which intervenes with healthy populations, secondary prevention involves some systematic screening or evaluation process to identify those in a population displaying early signs of dysfunction. Only individuals showing such difficulties are targeted for treatment. The basic goal of secondary prevention is to prevent serious maladjustment from occurring by helping those who have subclinical difficulties.

Sometimes it is difficult to tell if an intervention is a primary prevention high-risk approach or secondary prevention. Much depends on how carefully the researcher has screened the target population for the presence of problems. Nevertheless, both primary and secondary prevention are proactive, population-oriented approaches that occur before the onset of full-blown clinical disorders. The Institute of Medicine (1994) has recommended renaming the primary prevention high-risk approach and all forms of secondary prevention *selective* and *indicated* preventive interventions, respectively, but whether these terms will catch on is unknown. In this text I retain the use of the traditional terms, primary and secondary prevention, and discuss these approaches separately whenever it is possible to do so.

DIFFICULTIES IN DOING PREVENTION

Conceptual and Methodological Issues

There are several conceptual and methodological questions that must be answered before prevention programs can be maximally effective. For instance, those interested in health promotion must determine which core skills mediate adjustment. Investigators using an environmental approach must answer several questions: How should the environment be measured? How do individual and environmental characteristics interact? What is the best way to alter certain aspects of the environment? What is the best person-environment fit for different groups?

The appropriate selection of target groups for prevention also involves answers to some critical questions. Targeting high-risk groups in primary prevention involves determining the following: Who is at risk? How is risk manifested? What changes are needed in individuals, in environments, or in both to reduce risk? Working with individuals undergoing life transitions or stressful events requires an understanding of the developmental sequences and impacts of these occurrences for different groups. What events have important implications for adjustment and maladjustment? What negative outcomes result from different transitions, and how can mastery of these transitions be attained? Finally, secondary prevention requires effective and efficient mechanisms to identify early signs of dysfunction for different problems that might occur at different ages.

Finally, prevention would be much easier to do if the specific causes of different disorders were known and if there were a clear developmental history illustrating the evolution of different problems and competencies for different groups of children at different ages. Unfortunately, current information in each of the areas mentioned above is incomplete, and many important issues facing prevention have yet to be resolved (Heller, Price, & Sher, 1980; Institute of Medicine, 1994; Jansen & Johnson, 1993; Jason, Thompson, & Rose, 1986).

As the field awaits critical data on substantive theoretical and methodological issues, prevention research has evolved in two ways. First, investigators have widened the goals of prevention beyond the prevention of specific disorders to include the more general modification of behavioral and emotional problems. Moreover, evaluations have emphasized continuous rather than categorical outcome criteria. That is, instead of determining whether or not a disorder is present, many investigators have assessed the amount of change achieved by interventions. How have levels of problems or competencies changed? There is nothing inherently contradictory between categorical and continuous evaluation models, and the two can be merged for maximum information. In fact, given the limitations of current diagnostic systems for children, a continuous approach aids prevention research by assessing relative levels of adjustment and maladjustment.

Second, investigators have emphasized the importance of achieving proximal (immediate) as well as distal (long-term) program objectives. Although prevention over the long term is the ultimate goal, it is important to document that the intervention is on the right track by achieving immediate and shorter-term objectives. In the search for appropriate criteria by which to judge the value of preventions, many researchers have emphasized the importance of evaluating risk factors and protective factors. In fact, some writers now emphasize that prevention occurs through the modification of risk and protective factors in different populations (e.g., Coie et al., 1993; Hawkins, Catalano, & Miller, 1992; Institute of Medicine, 1994). The evolution of the literature on risk factors and protective factors is perhaps the most important recent development in prevention and deserves extended discussion.

Risk Factors and Protective Factors

Both risk factors and protective factors have influence on the probability of future outcomes. That is, a risk factor is anything that is associated with an increased likelihood of future negative outcomes. Most researchers conceive of protective factors in conjunction with pathology, by defining a protective factor as any variable that is associated with a decreased likelihood of negative outcomes. Protective factors may diminish problems directly or operate indirectly by interacting with risk factors to reduce problems or in some way to prevent the occurrence of risk factors. For example, protective factors may buffer individuals against stress, diminish the impact of stress, or prevent the occurrence of stress.

However, mental health is not the opposite of mental illness. The absence of problems does not mean that sufficient positive mental health skills, competencies, or coping resources are present. Therefore, it is possible to view a protective factor specifically in relation to mental health. A protective factor is any variable associated with an increased likelihood of *positive* outcomes. In other words, protective factors can also work directly to improve psychological well-being. Freeing protective factors from study within a pathological paradigm may help us to identify more protective factors. Researchers have identified many more risk factors than protective factors, perhaps because of an ingrained tendency to view development from a deficiency rather than a competency perspective.

Table 1.1 presents several emerging principles related to risk and protective factors. Several sources discuss these issues in more depth (Coie et al., 1993; Hawkins et al., 1992; Institute of Medicine, 1994; Rutter, 1994), but several comments are appropriate here.

A risk factor can be an attribute of an individual (e.g., lack of effective communication skills) or of the environment (e.g., friends who use drugs, or the lack of social support); it can be a demographic characteristic not easily changed (e.g., low-income status) or a behavior that is amenable to influence (e.g., unprotected sexual intercourse). Some risk factors are simultaneously predictors, consequences, and problems. For instance, early aggression in the first and second grades, which is a problem in and of itself, predicts later more serious aggression, but can be predicted by earlier noncompliance during the preschool years (McMahon, 1994). Risk factors and protective factors are not the converse of each other. Aggressive behavior is a risk factor, but lack of aggression is not a protective factor. Some risk variables are helpful in targeting a population for intervention (e.g., having an alcoholic parent) but do not help in explaining why precisely a particular group is at risk. Often such variables are called *marker variables, markers,* or *proxy variables.*

TABLE 1.1 Current Knowledge Regarding Risk and Protective Factors

1. There are multiple rather than single factors related to any one disorder or problem.
2. The same factor may be associated with more than one problem.
3. The effects of factors are often multiplicative rather than merely additive.
4. Many outcomes seem to be affected by both personal and environmental factors.
5. The mechanisms of action for factors are unknown.
6. We know much more about risk factors than about protective factors.
7. There is substantial heterogeneity in outcomes in relation to specific factors.
8. Different factors are important at different ages and under different circumstances.
9. We do not know all the relevant factors for different outcomes.

It is believed there are multiple risk factors for most problems. For instance, risk factors in the individual, family, peer group, school, and community are all associated with drug use (Hawkins et al., 1992). The implication is that interventions might have to target as many of these risk indices as possible in order to be effective. Furthermore, different risk factors are present within different groups of children (e.g., some adolescents have friends who misuse alcohol). The implication here is that a different intervention may be needed for different groups, depending on their level of risk.

As if the situation were not complicated enough, a single risk factor can be associated with several different problems. For instance, early poor academic achievement is a risk factor for later school failure, delinquency, drug use, and behavioral problems. Therefore, the elimination of academic deficiencies may reduce the likelihood of several different problems simultaneously. However, other factors—such as early behavior problems and poor peer relations—are also associated with the same later problems (Dryfoos, 1990). It is not clear how much unique variance in later outcomes is explained by each of these risk factors.

Our current knowledge of the complex relationships among risk factors, protective factors, and adjustment and maladjustment is limited. We do not know all the factors specific to each outcome or how they interact. It does seem that many risk factors have multiplicative rather than additive effects, and that in at least some cases, some unknown threshold must be passed before a risk factor begins to operate. For example, Rutter (1979) examined six risks associated with children's psychiatric disorders, such as severe marital discord and maternal psychiatric problems. Outcomes for children exposed to only one risk were similar to those for children exposed to none. Those exposed to two risk factors, however, were 4 times more likely to have clinical problems, and those exposed to four or more of the six were 20 times more likely to have difficulties.

Furthermore, we know little about the mechanisms of actions of different factors. For instance, children who have poor peer relations are at risk for a variety of later problems, but exactly why this is so is the subject of much current research (Asher & Coie, 1990). Risk factors also tend to change in salience over time. Reading problems that first appear in fifth grade are less serious than reading problems that first appear in first grade.

Finally, the relationships among risk factors, protective factors, and outcomes are far from perfect. Although some individuals may be at relatively higher risk than others, this in no way assures negative outcomes. For example, one study found that externalizing problems during preschool were the best predictor of conduct problems at age 11 (and thus a risk factor), but there was an 85% false positive hit rate (White, Moffitt, Earls, Robins, & Silva, 1990). In other words, 85% of preschoolers with problems did not have problems at age 11.

Risk factors and protective factors currently serve an important function in prevention research as proximal outcome criteria. If interventions reduce risk and increase protection among target groups, then it is reasonable to assume that future difficulties among the members of those groups are less likely and that the intervention has had a preventive effect. Ultimately, this assumption must be confirmed by follow-up studies, but immediate information on which risk factors and protective factors can be modified and which interventions are helpful in this regard is important for the improvement of the efficiency of prevention programs. Many areas of prevention discussed in this book can be viewed from a risk factor and protective factor paradigm.

Practical Impediments to Prevention

Some practical impediments to prevention are worth mentioning. School-based prevention is applied field research, and there are inherent difficulties involved in such activities. Basically, when investigators intervene in real-world settings they usually are unable to control every aspect of the research that might affect the conduct and outcome of an intervention. For example, researchers often cannot control completely who participates in the intervention, how individuals are assigned to conditions, the length or intensity of the program, what information can be collected to evaluate outcomes, and how often and when data can be obtained. Therefore, applied field research is almost always less than perfect. Investigators do the best they can under trying circumstances, take advantage of prior successes, learn from past mistakes, and hope that convergent replication of findings across settings and research groups will increase the interpretability of results.

In summary, there are several conceptual, methodological, and logistical issues that impede prevention research. Under the circumstances, one might assume that the field of school-based prevention has not advanced very far. In fact, this is not so. Many studies have reported positive results, and recent work is beginning to supply some of the pieces of information that researchers need to mount successively more rigorous and effective programs. It would be premature to declare that it is currently possible to prevent negative outcomes in schoolchildren, because the information we have is not definitive. Nevertheless, we are beginning to learn what works under different circumstances. It is my aim in this book to discuss these findings.

PREVENTION PROGRAMS IN SCHOOLS

Brief History of School-Based Prevention

Prevention in schools is not a new idea. Between 1920 and 1940 some prevention-oriented mental health programs were conducted in schools in conjunction with the child guidance clinic movement. Programs for high-risk children were developed, and formal classroom curricula to teach principles of mental hygiene were available in the early 1940s (Long, 1989). Although some of these early programs were popular, they were not formally evaluated. Similarly, some form of sex education has been conducted in schools for more than a century, and health education was begun in the early 1900s.

A few pioneering prevention studies appeared in the 1950s, such as the St. Louis Project (see Glidewell, Gildea, & Kaufman, 1973), but other evaluations were slow to appear. In contrast to its early history, school-based prevention has become very popular within the past few years. This is evident when we consider the current status of research and practice on prevention.

Research on Prevention

Figure 1.2 presents the number of published controlled outcome studies on school-based prevention that have appeared over 5-year time blocks,

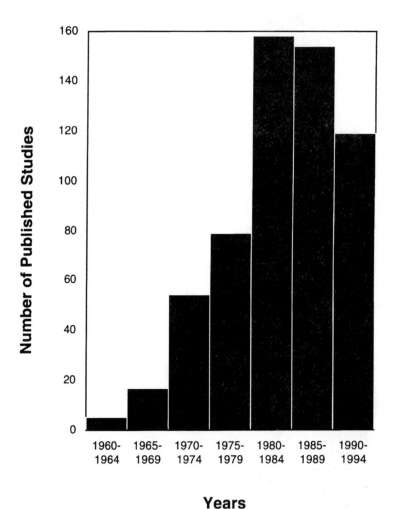

Figure 1.2. Number of Published Outcome Studies on School-Based Prevention That Have Appeared Since 1960

beginning in 1960, when research on the topic began appearing with some frequency. Only studies that evaluated preventive programs quantitatively and compared an intervention group with a comparison group are included. In other words, single-group pre/post designs, case reports, and qualitative analyses are not represented.

Figure 1.2 indicates that research on school-based prevention began slowly; only a few studies appeared during the 1960s. Published studies increased in frequency during the 1970s and accelerated rapidly in the 1980s. In fact, 74% of all published research on this topic has appeared since 1980. Overall, between 1960 and 1994, 586 published outcome studies of school-based prevention programs appeared. However, Figure 1.2 does not include programs designed to prevent academic problems. There have been several hundred published studies of early childhood education and approximately 500 studies of academic interventions at the elementary level, many of which are unpublished (Slavin, Karweit, & Madden, 1989; Slavin, Karweit, & Wasik, 1994).[1]

Practice of Prevention

Although the total number of controlled outcome studies on school-based prevention is impressive, the practice of prevention far surpasses the research base. Numerous preventive programs of all types are offered in schools each year. Surveys indicate that more than 70% of all school districts have curricula designed to prevent smoking, alcohol use, drug use, and physical health problems in children (Holtzman et al., 1992); 85% of schoolchildren receive some form of sex education (Alan Guttmacher Institute, 1994). One violence prevention program, Resolving Conflict Creatively, served 225 schools and reached 120,000 students in 1993 (Coben, Weiss, Mulvey, & Dearwater, 1994). Thus, as these figures indicate, each year millions of schoolchildren are exposed to prevention-oriented programs, and many participate in more than one.

Unfortunately, the great majority of school-based programs have never been evaluated in any systematic fashion, and the findings concerning those that have been assessed do not inspire much confidence in their effectiveness. Current school-based programs exist for a variety of political, administrative, and financial reasons. For example, many state departments of education mandate instruction concerning topics such as health, sex, drug abuse, and AIDS. As a result, in an effort to meet such requirements, schools may choose programs that are readily available and easy to implement. Funding also plays a role. For instance, Project DARE is believed to be the most widely used school-based drug-use prevention program in the United States; it has been adopted by approximately 50% of local school districts nationwide. Public funding for Project DARE, which is conducted by local law enforcement officials who lead classroom lesson plans, comes through the 1986 Drug-Free Schools and Communities Act. Despite the fact that Project DARE is so widely used, evidence fails to support the program's ability to modify student drug use (Ennett, Tobler, Ringwalt, & Flewelling, 1994).

The fact that the practice of school-based prevention has surpassed its scientific base is disconcerting. Many children are exposed to curricula the impacts of which are unknown. Nonetheless, the number of interventions regularly offered in schools represents an opportunity. Schools are a natural base for preventive programs, and school staff are willing to accommodate such programs, at least on a trial basis. Therefore, we need to understand what types of prevention programs work most effectively in the schools, for what populations, and to what ends. My aims in this text are to cover this territory and to summarize the current findings in school-based prevention.

A previous volume in the Sage Series on Developmental Clinical Psychology and Psychiatry authored by Rickel and Allen (1987) provides a broad overview of prevention, from infancy through adolescence, and discusses a few school-based programs and many community- and home-based interventions. There is now sufficient literature available describing school-based programs that this separate book is warranted. In this volume, I focus on the results of published outcome studies in order to discuss theory, research, and practice in school-based prevention. For the most part, I emphasize work in primary and secondary schools, although in Chapter 3 I discuss a few interventions begun in infancy and preschool to prevent later learning problems.

Because it is impossible to discuss all of the controlled outcome research that has appeared, I have carefully chosen the individual studies cited and discussed in this text as examples of the best work in each area. Generally, these investigations have obtained the most impressive results and at the same time have attended to many of the major methodological and conceptual issues confronting their respective research domains. Although exemplary investigations are in the minority, they serve as models for future work and suggest what can be accomplished when interventions are carefully conceptualized, conducted, and evaluated. Therefore, my intent is to highlight programs that appear to be the most successful, describing the principles that seem to account for this success whenever possible.

In the chapters that follow, I examine the research that has been conducted in several areas of prevention. This relatively comprehensive perspective on school-based prevention is preferable to a narrower focus for two important reasons. First, parochialism is present in much prevention research. Unfortunately, investigators seldom cite work outside their own areas, although there is much to be learned by considering the successes and failures of researchers in various disciplines. One good example is the initial emphasis on interventions that concentrated on dissemination of information. Each area of school-based prevention began with the assumption that increasing students' knowledge about preventive concepts would change their behavior. In every case, this has proven to be a false assumption. If researchers had been aware of previous findings from outside their own fields, they might not have wasted valuable time and effort on ineffective strategies.

A second benefit of synthesizing findings from different areas lies in the convergent validity that can accrue. When independent investigators using different methodologies, studying diverse populations, and attempting different goals nevertheless report similar findings and reach similar conclusions, confidence is increased that the programs in question have merit. This is beginning to happen in school-based prevention. Although there is still much to be learned, results are beginning to converge regarding the most promising preventive approaches.

PLAN OF THE BOOK

This book contains seven chapters. In this chapter, I have distinguished the different approaches taken in prevention, discussed some of the challenges and issues involved in conducting and evaluating interventions, and described the history and current status of prevention in the schools. In the next four chapters, I discuss programs in different areas. Chapter 2 is devoted to programs designed to prevent behavioral and social problems, a topic that conveniently divides into primary and secondary prevention. Findings from 261 programs are summarized. Chapter 3 presents a discussion of the prevention of substance abuse, and Chapter 4 evaluates research on the prevention of academic problems. Chapter 5 describes health education programs designed to improve the cardiovascular health of children in such areas as nutrition and physical fitness. AIDS, sex education, and pregnancy prevention programs are also addressed. Chapter 6 takes up the important topic of program diffusion, or the extent to which successful prevention programs are identified and used in the schools. Finally, in Chapter 7, I synthesize the information from the preceding chapters in an attempt to reach some general conclusions about the impacts of school-based prevention programs and to highlight how these programs can be made more efficient and effective.

SUMMARY

Our current mental health system is not reaching many children and adolescents who need help. Estimates suggest that at best only 10% to 30% of children with clinical-level dysfunction ever receive any treatment. Therefore, prevention programs can fill an important void by helping school-age children who will likely never receive any formal mental health care. There are two major types of prevention, primary and secondary, and each is a proactive, population-oriented approach that occurs before the onset of full-blown disorders. Primary prevention involves a collection of strategies that attempt to prevent problems from developing in currently normal populations by changing the environment, by changing individuals, or by doing both, including attempts at mental health promotion. Secondary prevention is prompt intervention with individuals displaying subclinical-level problems. This book highlights successful primary and secondary prevention programs in several different areas in an attempt to summarize the current status of theory, research, and practice in school-based prevention.

NOTE

1. In conducting the search for studies to include in Figure 1.2, I depended on several published reviews of prevention research, my own knowledge of the literature, and a research bibliography obtained from the Institute of Medicine. Only work appearing in English-language journals was included. Although the literature search was not exhaustive, most relevant studies were probably counted. Although exact figures are not available, there have probably been half as many unpublished studies evaluating nonacademic preventive programs as there have been published reports. This estimate is based on some unpublished work of my own, in which my colleagues and I sought to estimate how many unpublished studies have assessed prevention programs (Durlak, Lampman, Wells, & Cotten, 1993). The relative dip in the number of published articles appearing in the period 1990-1994 compared with the two earlier 5-year time blocks is due, in part, to the fact that not all 1994 studies were counted. This book was being finished at the end of 1994, and the year-end issues of many journals had not yet appeared.

2

PREVENTION OF BEHAVIORAL AND SOCIAL PROBLEMS

THE NEED FOR PREVENTIVE SERVICES

Although there is no standardized reporting system, information summarized by Knitzer, Steinberg, and Fleisch (1990) suggests that relatively few maladapting schoolchildren receive school-based mental health care and that those who do receive services that are neither lengthy nor timely. For instance, although up to 15% of schoolchildren experience clinical-level dysfunction, schools formally designate only 1% of the school population as having serious problems, labeling them behaviorally or emotionally disturbed. Only two thirds to three fourths of these children receive any school mental health services, and less than half receive more than five sessions a year. Finally, although most children with serious problems are identified in the early primary grades, the majority who receive any mental health treatment are between 12 and 16 years old. Programs to prevent behavioral and social maladjustment could fill an important need by helping many school-age children who will likely never receive any mental health care.

This chapter is devoted to discussion of programs designed to prevent behavioral and social problems. In this area it is possible to discuss primary and secondary prevention programs separately, because researchers have tended to target either children with no known problems (primary prevention) or those beginning to show early signs of difficulty (secondary prevention).

PRIMARY PREVENTION

Durlak, Lampman, Wells, and Cotten (1993) conducted a meta-analysis evaluating controlled outcome studies of primary prevention that had appeared through the end of 1991. The major findings for the 131 school-based programs in this review are presented in Table 2.1. Results for different types of programs are expressed in terms of mean effect sizes (ESs), which are standardized mean differences comparing the postintervention statuses of experimental and control groups. In brief, an ES reflects how much change has occurred from an intervention; higher numbers indicate stronger program impact. The appendix to this volume presents a brief explanation of ESs and their interpretation.

In general, all types of programs had significant positive impacts on participants; the mean ESs ranged from 0.25 to 0.50. It is helpful to compare these outcomes with those obtained from other types of treatments. Lipsey and Wilson (1993) report that the mean ES obtained from 156 different meta-analyses evaluating various social, behavioral, and educational treatments was 0.47 ($SD = 0.28$). The results obtained for primary prevention programs are within this range. Compared with treatments for dysfunctional children, slightly lower mean effects can be expected for primary prevention programs, because children in such programs are initially functioning within the normal range.

Table 2.1 also presents mean ESs expressed in terms of either assessed competencies or problems. Outcomes assessing problems would include symptom checklists, self-reports of anxiety, and observations of inappropriate behavior; those evaluating competence would focus on assertiveness, interpersonal problem-solving skills, increases in self-esteem or self-efficacy, and so on. With the exception of problem-solving interventions, programs produced similar and significant effects on both competencies and problems. In other words, primary prevention programs had the dual effect of improving participants' status on indicators of both adjustment and maladjustment.

Competency enhancement coupled with a reduction in problems has important preventive implications. For example, a program that ends with participants having greater self-confidence and better coping abilities would seem to place participants at lower risk for future problems than a program that only reduces pathology.

Although outcome data for primary prevention programs are generally positive, conclusions about program impact are offered cautiously for two main reasons. First, only a minority of programs collected follow-up data

TABLE 2.1 Mean Effect Sizes for Primary Prevention Programs to Prevent Behavioral and Social Problems

Type of Program (no. of studies)	All Outcomes	Mean Effect Size Competencies	Problems
Environmental programs (17)	0.35	0.56	0.26
Transition programs			
divorce (7)	0.36	0.33	0.38
school entry/change (9)	0.39	0.41	0.36
Person-centered programs			
affective education (46)	0.29	0.31	0.26
interpersonal problem solving (23)	0.39	0.44	0.06[a]
Other programs			
behavioral (26)	0.50	0.44	0.55
nonbehavioral (16)	0.25	0.24	0.25

SOURCE: Data are drawn from Durlak et al. (1993).
NOTE: a. Only mean effect *not* significantly different from zero.

(26%), and follow-up periods were relatively short in many cases. The median follow-up period was only 8 weeks, and only eight studies collected follow-up data at 1 year or later. Therefore, the durability of program impact for many interventions is largely unknown. Second, in several cases there was a failure to formulate and test specific hypotheses. For example, researchers have not always articulated specific program objectives or presented theory-based rationales for why interventions should achieve certain outcomes. The presence of vague goals (e.g., "to prevent school maladjustment") coupled with the use of measures that assess general aspects of functioning (e.g., self-esteem or anxiety) makes it difficult to interpret an intervention's preventive impact. There are significant exceptions to the above, however, and some exemplary programs that offer the strongest evidence for preventive effects are described in the following sections. Different types of interventions are presented below using the conceptual distinctions discussed in Chapter 1.

Person-Centered Approaches

Mental health promotion. One strategy in primary prevention involves health promotion, and two groups of studies fit this mold: those involving affective education and those involving interpersonal problem-solving training. Programs involving affective education represent a diverse set of interventions that share the common goal of emotional and social growth. The general intent of these programs is to improve children's adjustment by increasing their self-understanding and self-acceptance, and by helping them understand factors that influence their own and others' feelings and behaviors. The availability of commercial programs and the intuitive appeal of this approach for teachers have made affective education very popular in the schools. Lesson plans and units are available for early and middle elementary students that combine puppet play, music, stories, group discussions, and various exercises.

For example, DeCharms (1972) trained teachers in affective education techniques in an attempt to influence African American sixth- and seventh-grade children to (a) become aware of their personal strengths and weaknesses, (b) understand the motivations behind their own and others' behaviors, and (c) establish realistic personal goals. Student data indicated that trained teachers created a classroom climate that fostered the development of these goals—that is, that encouraged self-study and personal goal setting. School data indicated improvement in both academic achievement and school attendance as a result of the intervention.

The interpersonal problem-solving approach has been promoted by Spivack and Shure (1974), who assert that cognitively based problem-solving skills mediate interpersonal adjustment. These skills include the ability (a) to recognize the existence of interpersonal problems, (b) to generate appropriate solutions to problems, and (c) to anticipate the consequences of different solutions. The data displayed in Table 2.1 indicate that problem-solving programs did significantly increase competencies (mean ES = 0.44), but were the only type of intervention that was not effective in changing problems (mean ES = 0.06, *ns*). Therefore, the link between the promotion of problem-solving skills and the prevention of problems has not been demonstrated. Nevertheless, problem-solving training has been incorporated as an element in several multidimensional programs that have had positive results (e.g., Hawkins, Von Cleve, & Catalano, 1991). Perhaps problem-solving training by itself is not effective but does work when combined with other components. The relative contribution of problem-solving components in multidimensional programs needs to be investigated in future research.

Additional analyses have suggested that both affective education and problem-solving programs are more effective for younger children. Children ages 4 to 7 have been found to have changed the most (effect sizes of 0.70 and 0.93, respectively), whereas effects for older children have been only one third as high. These interventions may be better suited for younger children, or it might be that the programs need to be modified to be more helpful for children at higher cognitive developmental levels.

Other programs. Finally, a relatively large number of person-centered primary prevention studies were difficult to categorize because of the diversity of techniques, objectives, and procedures used. Some programs sought to prevent specific problems, others attempted to reduce risk factors, and still others were health promotion efforts targeting different competencies (e.g., self-esteem, communication skills, assertiveness). Analysis indicated that the use of behavioral or nonbehavioral change strategies was more important than any other variable in affecting outcomes. Programs using the former techniques obtained effects twice as large as those using the latter (ESs of 0.50 versus 0.26). Behavioral procedures tended to involve reinforcement, modeling, and cognitive self-control techniques, whereas nonbehavioral procedures typically included nondirective forms of group discussion and interaction. The fact that behavioral approaches to skills training were effective is not surprising. Similar results have been obtained for prevention programs related to drug use (see Chapter 3) and health education (see Chapter 5).

Interventions developed by Hartman and by Digiuseppe and Kassinove illustrate successful behavioral programs. Hartman (1979) classified high school students as being at low or high risk for subsequent psychological problems according to the results of a test battery that assessed the amount of stress experienced by these students as well as the extent and quality of their coping skills. A high school teacher then taught the students various coping techniques, emphasizing cognitive restructuring, assertiveness, anxiety management, and social skills training. At the end of the 8-week class and at 3-month follow-up, the intervention produced significant changes in psychological functioning for all students compared with controls, and was relatively more helpful for those initially at higher risk. Digiuseppe and Kassinove (1976) reported that a 15-week rational emotive therapy approach was successful in modifying the irrational beliefs held by fourth and eight graders. Children also reported less anxiety and fewer neurotic symptoms following the intervention. An alternate program emphasizing psychodynamic principles was not effective in improving children's adjustment.

Transition or Milestone Programs

There are two types of school-based transition programs: those designed for children of divorcing parents and those designed for children who are changing schools. The potential negative effects of divorce on children are well known (Emery, 1988). Programs for children of divorce adapt a variety of clinical techniques to help children deal with the stress of divorce. Opportunities for discussion, ventilation of feelings, and social support are provided, usually in a group context (e.g., Alpert-Gillis, Pedro-Carroll, & Cowen, 1989).

Because at least one third of all children will eventually experience the divorce of their parents, and in growing recognition that divorce can have negative effects on children's peer relations, school achievement, and personality functioning, interventions for children of divorce are becoming increasingly popular in the schools. Emery (1988) and Grych and Fincham (1992) offer excellent overviews of the issues involved in implementing and evaluating such interventions.

Children who must change schools represent another opportunity for primary prevention interventions. Approximately 6 million students (ages 5-13) change schools each year, and it is believed that many of them experience some difficulty in adjusting (Jason et al., 1992). Jason et al. (1992) have summarized findings from their School Transition Project, an attempt to help high-risk multiethnic middle school children (Grades 4-6) who were entering new inner-city schools. In successive studies, children considered to be at academic risk on the basis of low standardized achievement scores received an orientation program conducted by a sixth-grade peer and in-school academic tutoring during the new school year from college undergraduates or home tutoring from trained parents. In Study 1, experimental children improved significantly in achievement scores compared with controls, and 50% more experimental than control children moved out of the academic at-risk category. In Study 2, tutored children in both conditions again demonstrated academic gains and parent tutoring produced more favorable results on measures of classroom social behavior than in-school tutoring. Finally, 1-year follow-up of the first cohort indicated that experimental children had maintained their academic gains.

Environmental Programs

Although programs attempting environmental changes are in the minority ($n = 17$), the results of several interventions have been particularly impressive. For example, attempts at changing a school's psychosocial environment to increase peer and teacher support for low-income, multi-ethnic students have been successful (Felner & Adan, 1988). Instead of frequently changing classes and teachers, program students were kept together for core academic subjects. These students were in homerooms in which assigned teachers were trained to function as counselors and to offer social support for school-related difficulties. Significant program effects were obtained for grades, school attendance, self-concept, and positive perceptions of the school environment. A 3-year follow-up indicated significantly higher grades and lower absenteeism for program students and a 48% lower school dropout rate.

Weinstein et al. (1991) also successfully changed the school environment through a multicomponent intervention that focused on eight school features, including curricula, student ability groupings, evaluation procedures, teacher-student relationships, and parent involvement. At-risk, multiethnic high school students changed significantly in grades, disciplinary referrals, and school absences compared with controls, and at 1-year follow-up had a 50% lower school dropout rate.

Hawkins et al. (1991) sought to prevent aggression and other acting-out behaviors by changing both the classroom and home environments of subjects in a program that combined teacher and parent interventions. Parents of low-income multiethnic children entering first grade received training in behavioral management practices for use in the home. Teachers were trained in proactive classroom management (see Chapter 4) and in specific interactive teaching methods. The latter included changing several instructional procedures in the class so that teachers monitored and reinforced student progress on individually paced academic tasks. Children were also trained in interpersonal problem-solving skills by their teachers. Compared with controls, experimental boys were significantly less aggressive and experimental girls were significantly less self-destructive, according to teacher ratings. Only 6% of experimental boys, compared with 20% of control boys, were in the clinical range of dysfunction on aggressive behavior.

Finally, the Houston Program (Johnson, 1988), which targeted low-income Mexican American families, is an example of environmental change occurring during early childhood. In this case, the multicomponent intervention involved the creation of a new setting, a child development center offering services to the entire family. The program, which began when the child was 1 year old, involved biweekly home visits and weekend sessions conducted by a paraprofessional child educator. These visits focused on issues related to parent-child interactions and early child development.

English-language classes and homemaking services were also offered to the parents. Families began visiting the child development center when the child was 2 years old. At the center, parents learned child-rearing techniques, were offered social support, and were generally empowered to seek necessary medical, social, and vocational services for themselves and their family members. The total program involved approximately 500 hours of participants' time over a 2-year period.

One goal of the Houston Program was to prevent subsequent behavior problems in school. Evaluations have indicated that parents demonstrated changes in several targeted child-rearing and social interaction skills, and children showed improved cognitive development. Long-term follow-up when children were in Grades 2 through 5, that is, 5 to 8 years after the intervention formally ended, indicated that teachers reported significantly fewer acting-out and aggressive problems in program children than in controls.

Additional Studies

A few findings appearing after Durlak et al.'s (1993) review warrant attention. First, research groups are beginning to replicate their earlier programs successfully, lending more confidence to the obtained findings (e.g., Felner et al., 1993; O'Donnell, Hawkins, Catalano, Abbott, & Day, 1995). Second, two projects attempting the prevention of aggression behaviors have reported positive results. The first project used a teacher-administered group contingency technique, the Good Behavior Game, over a 2-year period to reduce aggressive behavior in first-grade children (Kellam, Rebok, Ialongo, & Mayer, 1994). The Good Behavior Game has been used in several behavioral treatments to reduce disruptive classroom behavior, and Kellam et al. (1994) have demonstrated its potential as a preventive intervention. Analyses indicated that a significant overall reduction in aggressive behavior was maintained over a 4-year follow-up period. Moreover, the intervention was more successful for those children at highest risk—that is, for those with initially higher levels of aggressive behavior in first grade.

The second project reported success in modifying bullying, a form of aggressive behavior in which children are physically or verbally intimidated or victimized by their peers (Olweus, 1993). In general, the program emphasized careful monitoring of peer behavior, with immediate non-physical sanctions for rule violations coupled with reinforcing contact between adults and children for positive behavior. A school program was established that combined intervention at the individual, classroom, and schoolwide levels. For example, school assemblies and teacher conferences were held to discuss the problem and its possible solution, children caught bullying were counseled and consultation was offered to their parents, class rules were established prohibiting aggressive behavior, and class meetings were held to discuss incidents. The program resulted in a substantial reduction of bullying and other antisocial behaviors, more positive attitudes toward school, and several indications of improvement in the social climate of the school.

In summary, programs to prevent behavioral and social problems have generally been successful in improving competencies and reducing problems. Positive outcomes have been obtained for several different types of programs, including person- and environment-centered programs and interventions for children undergoing transitions. Unfortunately, relatively few programs have examined the durability of outcomes. The most impressive evidence for preventive effects has come from programs obtaining change on such indices of adjustment as levels of aggressive behavior, grades, and school dropout rates. Many of these successful interventions have modified the school environment. The relative effectiveness of different features of these multicomponent interventions should be explored.

SECONDARY PREVENTION

Secondary prevention programs (or indicated preventive interventions) provide prompt intervention for problems that are detected early; they typically operate as follows. A particular population in one or more schools (e.g., all first graders, all those in junior high) is screened or evaluated in some way and criteria are used to target some for intervention, which follows quickly after the collection of more information confirming the nature of the children's difficulties. The intent of secondary prevention is to help children with subclinical problems so that they avoid developing full-blown disorders. It is believed that the earlier the intervention occurs, the greater the likelihood of success. In other words, it makes sense to intervene when problems are just beginning rather than to wait for them to intensify over time.

There are two main aspects to secondary prevention programs. The first involves the early identification of school problems; the second involves the treatment provided to target children. Each of these aspects is discussed below.

Identifying School Maladjustment

Currently, there is no standardized approach for detecting early signs of school maladjustment. Investigators have used different procedures, depending on the problem of interest. Table 2.2 provides examples from representative programs. For instance, investigators frequently ask teachers to rate students on one or more scales to detect behavioral problems. Teacher ratings, however, may overlook children with internalizing difficulties. To identify specific internalizing problems, such as depression or anxiety, researchers may administer self-report inventories to children. To assess peer relations, researchers may use sociometric procedures to discern which children have high or low rates of peer acceptance. Any of these screening methods can be complemented by additional assessment techniques, including various observational procedures.

The accurate identification of early signs of school maladjustment is a sensitive undertaking. On the one hand, because only some children are singled out for intervention, there is always the possibility of stigmatizing these children and creating negative expectations regarding their behavior. On the other hand, children's problems must be identified before they can be resolved.

Screening techniques must be not only accurate and reliable, but quick and user-friendly. Overly complicated and burdensome procedures are unlikely to be widely used in the schools. The screening instrument that has received the most attention to date is the AML, a brief teacher rating scale that assesses internalizing and externalizing behavior problems as well as learning difficulties (Cowen et al., 1973). Several lines of evidence indicate that the AML is a useful screening measure. In particular, acceptable hit rates have been achieved using the AML: between 86% and 93% of children with high AML scores have been independently confirmed using other criteria to have school adjustment problems (Durlak & Jason, 1984). It is not clear, however, how many false negatives occur as a result of AML screening—that is, how many children who do not receive high ratings from teachers are actually having problems in school.

Beyond the AML, few screening procedures have received much systematic research attention. The multistage screening process employed by some investigators to assess depression (Kahn, Kehle, Jenson, & Clark,

TABLE 2.2 Examples of Screening Methods in Secondary Prevention
Programs

Program	Target Group	Problem	Primary Screening Method
Camp, Blom, Herbert, & Van Doorninck (1977)	Grades 1-2	aggression	teacher ratings
Cowen (1980)	Grades K-3	behavior and learning difficulties	teacher ratings, brief psychological evaluations, interviews, case conferences
Wilson & Rotter (1986)	Grades 6-8	test anxiety	self-report
Kirschenbaum, DeVoge, Marsh, & Steffen (1980)	Grades 1-3	behavior problems of all types	teacher ratings, interviews, classroom observations
Lochman, Burch, Curry, & Lampron (1984)	Grades 4-6	aggression	teacher ratings
Oden & Asher (1977)	Grades 3-4	peer acceptance	sociometric: roster and rating task
Durlak (1977)	Grades 1-3	behavior problems of all types	teacher ratings, interviews
La Greca & Santogrossi (1980)	Grades 3-5	peer acceptance	sociometric: peer nomination
Kahn, Kehle, Jenson, & Clark (1990)	Grades 6-8	depression	three-stage process: self-report, self-report repeated, child interview
Stark, Reynolds, & Kaslow (1987)	Grades 4-6	depression	three-stage process: self-report, self-report repeated, child interview

1990; Stark, Reynolds, & Kaslow, 1987) is likely to be successful in
identifying children who are truly depressed, but it is not known how
many children are missed in the first round of screening.

Investigators have used different procedures in assessing peer status.
When using a roster and rating task (e.g., Oden & Asher, 1977), every

child is rated on every item by every other child, so that complete data are obtained for all children. Peer nomination procedures (e.g., La Greca & Santogrossi, 1980) typically ask children to list only their top three choices regarding others with whom they wish to play or work. Children not appearing among the top three rating categories are not necessarily unaccepted by their peers, however; they simply are not the most popular children. Asher and Coie (1990) discuss the interpretive and methodological issues involved in the assessment of peer relations. In summary, there is a need to evaluate how well screening procedures can detect different forms of early school dysfunction in a valid and economical fashion.

Secondary Prevention Programs

A few examples illustrate the diversity of procedures used in secondary prevention programs. The best-known secondary prevention program is the Primary Mental Health Project (PMHP) begun by Cowen and his colleagues in Rochester, New York, in 1957 (see Cowen, 1980). So called because of its focus on the primary (early elementary) school grades and not because it is a primary prevention program, the PMHP basically offers individual relationship-oriented (nonbehavioral) treatment to children who have externalizing or internalizing problems as well as learning difficulties. Trained homemakers have been the major therapeutic agents.

Other programs have used social and token reinforcement to modify children's acting-out and shy/withdrawn behaviors (Durlak, 1977; Kirschenbaum, DeVoge, Marsh, & Steffen, 1980). Cognitive-behavioral therapy techniques emphasizing self-monitoring and self-control have been used effectively to reduce aggressive behavior (Camp, Blom, Herbert, & Van Doorninck, 1977; Lochman, Burch, Curry, & Lampron, 1984) and depressive symptomatology (Kahn et al., 1990). La Greca and Santogrossi (1980) used social learning procedures to train social isolates in skills designed to increase their rates of peer acceptance. In a frequently cited study, Oden and Asher (1977) found it was possible to coach socially isolated children on how to improve their peer interactions. Most of the above interventions have been offered in group formats, have been relatively brief (12 or fewer sessions), and have successfully used a variety of change agents, such as teachers (Camp et al., 1977), school counselors (Durlak, 1977; Kahn et al., 1990), and graduate and undergraduate students (Kirschenbaum et al., 1980; La Greca & Santogrossi, 1980; Lochman et al., 1984; Oden & Asher, 1977).

Program Outcomes

Durlak and Wells (1994) conducted a meta-analytic review of the impact of secondary prevention by evaluating the results of 130 published and unpublished controlled outcome studies appearing by the end of 1991. All of these studies used person-centered approaches, and most (94%) were conducted in schools. As the findings did not vary when the few nonschool programs were removed, results for the complete review are discussed here. Programs focused strictly on academic remediation and those to prevent drug taking were not included, but such programs are discussed in Chapters 3 and 4.

The design of secondary prevention programs varied widely. For example, a relatively high percentage of studies randomly assigned participants to treatment and control conditions (71%), used multiple outcome measures (91%), and had low attrition (76%). In contrast, relatively few designs included attention placebo controls (28%), collected follow-up data (29%), or used normed outcome measures (20%). None of the above procedures was significantly related to program outcomes, but the data reported above indicate how methodological improvements can be made in future studies.

Table 2.3 summarizes the main findings from this meta-analysis. Results are presented first for the general type of treatment used, which was the most important factor affecting outcomes. Behavioral and cognitive-behavioral treatments were equally effective in producing moderately strong effects (mean ES of 0.51 and 0.53, respectively), which were almost twice as high as those emanating from nonbehavioral interventions (mean ES = 0.27).

The effectiveness in treating different types of presenting problems is also indicated in Table 2.3. Surprisingly, programs targeting externalizing problems achieved the highest effects (mean ES = 0.72). This category included aggression and other forms of acting-out problems. Loeber (1990) has indicated that the possibility of modifying acting-out behaviors decreases with age. Therefore, prompt intervention for dysfunction detected early might be responsible for the ability of secondary prevention to reduce acting-out behaviors.

The most common internalizing problems treated in secondary prevention programs have been anxiety and depression, which appear amenable to early intervention (mean ES = 0.49). Although the effects for children with academic problems and poor peer relations are more modest (ESs of 0.26 and 0.30, respectively), each of these dimensions is predictive of later

TABLE 2.3 Major Findings for Secondary Prevention Programs

	Mean Effect Size
Type of Treatment	
behavioral (*n* = 46)	0.51
cognitive-behavioral (*n* = 31)	0.53
nonbehavioral (*n* = 53)	0.27
Presenting Problem	
externalizing (*n* = 10)	0.72
internalizing (*n* = 38)	0.49
mixed symptomatology (*n* = 36)	0.38
poor academic achievement (*n* = 24)	0.26
poor peer relations (*n* = 21)	0.30

Results for Follow-Up Studies	*Postintervention*	*Follow-Up*	*Follow-Up Period (months)*
Behavioral (*n* = 12)	0.54	0.47	5
Cognitive-behavioral (*n* = 12)	0.80	0.84	3
Nonbehavioral (*n* = 11)	0.09	0.11	24

SOURCE: Data are drawn from Durlak and Wells (1994).
NOTE: *n* = number of studies.

adjustment, so that even modest changes on these indices can have some preventive impact.

The bottom of Table 2.3 summarizes follow-up data for secondary prevention programs. The results are encouraging, given that there is no lessening of program impact over time; however, only 29% of all programs collected follow-up information and the follow-up period was relatively short in most cases.

Finally, in a fashion similar to the findings for primary prevention, ESs were analyzed separately for outcome measures assessing competencies and problems. Although behavioral treatment produced higher effects than nonbehavioral interventions, both treatments were similar in ability to modify problems or competencies (mean ESs = 0.46 and 0.44 for behavioral treatment and 0.20 and 0.24 for nonbehavioral treatment, respectively). Cognitive-behavioral treatment did enhance competencies (mean ES = 0.39), but obtained much higher effects in terms of reducing problems (mean ES = 0.84).

In summary, results from 130 controlled outcome studies provide strong support for a secondary prevention model emphasizing timely intervention for subclinical problems detected early. Secondary prevention is applicable across a wide range of school settings, is appropriate for several different forms of dysfunction, and can be delivered in individual or group formats by diverse change agents. Various clinical procedures can be easily adapted once children in need of treatment are identified. Outcomes vary according to the type of treatment and presenting problem. In general, the best results are obtained for cognitive-behavioral and behavioral treatments and interventions targeting externalizing problems.

Additional Studies

Durlak and Wells (1994) reviewed secondary prevention programs that had been reported by the end of 1991. Studies appearing after this date have continued to support the efficacy of early intervention. In particular, three additional studies, all containing follow-up data, have been successful in reducing aggressive behavior in young children. For instance, Prinz, Blechman, and Dumas (1994) selected children from Grades 1 through 3 who obtained high aggression scores on a teacher-completed child behavior checklist. These children received weekly training for a full school year in various methods of prosocial coping. The intervention was effective in reducing teacher-rated aggressive behavior and in improving children's social skills, as assessed by both teachers and independent raters. These results were maintained at 6-month follow-up.

A second study also reported success in teaching social skills and cognitive-behavioral self-control techniques to aggressive children (Lochman, Coie, Underwood, & Terry, 1993). A combination of individual and group sessions was used with fourth-grade African American children who were aggressive and also socially rejected according to peer nomination ratings. At posttreatment, treated children had improved significantly in terms of both aggression and peer acceptance. At 1-year follow-up, treated children were still significantly less aggressive than control children; they also tended to be more accepted by their peers, but this latter finding fell short of traditional levels of statistical significance ($p < .08$).

Finally, a third study combined parent and child training in a successful effort to prevent disruptive behavior in white children from low-income families (Tremblay et al., 1992). Kindergarten teacher ratings identified children who exhibited disruptive behaviors (fighting, oppositionality, and hyperactivity). Parents were trained in behavior management strategies over a 2-year period, when the children were in first and second grades. Concurrent with the parent sessions, the children received training in social skills and self-control techniques at school. Coaching, modeling, behavioral rehearsal, and reinforcement were used. A 3-year follow-up indicated significantly less fighting and significantly better school achievement in the treated group. A global index of adjustment derived at follow-up indicated there were half as many boys with serious behavior problems in the treatment as in the no-treatment group (22% vs. 44%). Furthermore, approximately 50% more of the treated than control children were considered to be well adjusted (29% vs. 19%). Thus, recent studies add further support to the conclusion that secondary prevention can reduce aggressive behavior in young children.

OVERVIEW OF
PRIMARY AND SECONDARY PREVENTION

Methodological Issues

The designs of primary and secondary prevention programs share several positive features, but they also have some limitations. A majority of researchers have used randomized experimental designs and multiple outcome measures to assess change, and have not suffered much attrition in their study samples. Studies can be improved through the use of more normed outcome measures, identification of the active ingredients of treatments, and determination of how program effects generalize across settings, behaviors, and time. It is also important to determine which children display the most and least benefits from intervention in order to make current programs more efficient and effective. For secondary prevention, researchers need screening procedures that will allow them to identify early forms of dysfunction accurately and economically, so that they can assess different problems at different ages. For primary prevention, more theory-driven research is needed that specifies why and how a particular intervention will work to achieve different outcomes for different target groups.

Outcomes

Perhaps the most impressive finding from both primary and secondary prevention programs has been the success attained in modifying aggression and other forms of acting-out or disruptive behavior. Although most studies have been short-term interventions involving small samples, data continue to accumulate that prevention of acting-out behavior is possible through early intervention. The successful modification of these problems has important implications. Early acting-out problems have been related to many different types of later maladjustment, including conduct disorder, academic underachievement, substance abuse, and delinquency. Moreover, disruptive behaviors are traditionally the most intractable forms of childhood and adolescent dysfunction (Dumas, 1989; Kazdin, 1987). Therefore, the prevention of acting-out problems has clear practical significance and might reduce the ultimate extent or severity of several other forms of child and adolescent maladjustment. A large-scale, multisite collaborative research trial designed to prevent conduct disorders through early school- and home-based intervention is currently under way (Conduct Problems Prevention Research Group, 1992). The results of this carefully planned intervention, which should begin appearing soon, will provide valuable information on the early development and modification of externalizing problems.

SUMMARY

Outcome data indicate that both primary and secondary prevention works in the sense that participants display increased competencies and reduced problems following intervention, although the durability of these effects needs to be demonstrated in more studies. Several primary prevention programs that have attempted to influence children indirectly by modifying aspects of the school environment have been successful, but similar approaches have not been tried in secondary prevention.

3

SUBSTANCE USE

SCOPE OF THE PROBLEM

Problems related to drugs are a major problem in the United States. The total cost of alcohol and drug abuse is estimated to exceed $110 billion each year (National Commission on Children, 1991). Many school-aged children and adolescents experiment with drugs, and the eventual use and misuse of drugs can cause serious health, personal, and social problems. Surveys suggest that 1 in 20 high school seniors drink alcohol daily, and up to 1 in 3 report at least one episode of binge drinking in a 2-week period; approximately 1 in 12 students smoke at least a half a pack of cigarettes daily (Johnston, O'Malley, & Bachman, 1986). Youth who become psychologically or physically dependent on drugs or who misuse drugs or place themselves at risk because of drug use (e.g., driving while intoxicated) are of particular concern.

Prevention of drug use requires consideration. Treatments for individuals who have established habits of drug taking typically meet with limited success, and relapse is high (Schinke, Botvin, & Orlandi, 1991). Therefore, it makes sense to intervene to temper drug use among schoolchildren.

DRUG PROGRAMS IN SCHOOLS

Drug programs are the most prevalent of all school-based preventive interventions. Most school districts have incorporated some type of drug education and prevention programs as a regular part of the curriculum. Many schools either develop their own curricula or adopt commercially available programs (Bosworth & Sailes, 1993), and few of these programs are ever evaluated in any systematic fashion. Most currently used programs are educational in nature and their impact is dubious, but they are used because of their emotional appeal, because they are easy to admin-

ister, or in response to federal or state mandates for some type of instruction relative to drugs. The availability of funds is another inducement for
schools to choose certain programs. For instance, the most widely used
school-based program, Project DARE, a federally funded program conducted by police officers, has been used in more than 50% of all school
districts (Ennett, Tobler, Ringwalt, & Flewelling, 1994). Unfortunately,
controlled evaluations of DARE indicate the program does not significantly alter student drug use (Ennett et al., 1994).

A BRIEF HISTORY OF RESEARCH ON DRUG PROGRAMS

Many researcher-initiated drug programs have been evaluated. The
history of research on these programs discloses a rapid progression in
theoretical and methodological sophistication and a concomitant increase
in positive results for interventions. For example, early school-based
interventions had little behavioral impact on drug use (see Bangert-
Drowns, 1988; Dielman, 1994; Tobler, 1986). Most of these early interventions were informational programs that focused on providing students
with accurate information about drugs and the consequences of drug use.
It was assumed that such programs would change students' attitudes about
drugs, which, in turn, would influence their subsequent behavior. This
theory has been soundly discredited. The general consensus is that relying
upon knowledge alone to change behavior concerning drugs is misguided
(Dielman, 1994; Montagne & Scott, 1993; Schinke et al., 1991; Tobler,
1986).

Some early findings did suggest that psychosocial interventions could
be effective, however, and this possibility stimulated substantial interest
in such programs. In general, psychosocial programs emphasize environmental factors related to the family, peers, the media, and the broader
community that influence drug use. The second and third generations of
research projects generally confirmed that psychosocial programs had
significant immediate impact on drug taking (Bruvold, 1993; Flay, 1985;
Hansen, 1992; Tobler, 1986). The practical significance of these changes
and their durability over time, however, were open to question. Other
limitations among studies appeared in terms of both internal and external
validity. For example, attrition was high in some programs, most investigators depended on self-reports, mainly white middle-class samples were
studied, tobacco was the main target of intervention, follow-up was

lacking, or postprogram effects were not durable over time (see Dielman, 1994; Flay, 1985).

In the fourth and fifth waves of research, several investigators have responded to the above concerns and have produced a body of work that is impressive in both its scope and impact. Although all methodological and conceptual issues have not been resolved, more rigorously conducted evaluations have increased confidence in the general value of psychosocial interventions.

CONTEMPORARY PSYCHOSOCIAL PROGRAMS

Two general types of successful psychosocial programs have been developed: skills-training programs and comprehensive community efforts. Table 3.1 lists some characteristics and outcomes of several exemplary outcome studies in these areas. These studies were chosen to represent findings from programmatic research programs. In these programs, successive refinements and replications have been conducted across multiple sites or cohorts to assess each intervention. Collectively, the studies listed in Table 3.1 are theory driven; involve large multisite, often diverse, samples; use careful analytic procedures; check for program implementation; and collect follow-up data. However, not every study possesses each of these features.

Skills-Training Programs

There are two types of skills-training programs: One type focuses on the teaching of specific peer and social resistance skills, whereas the other focuses on general life skills. The former programs (often called resistance or refusal skills programs) attempt to develop skills specifically relevant to the resistance of peer and social pressure related to drug use, such as assertiveness and effective communication skills.

Resistance skills programs are based on the assumption that students must learn how to resist social and interpersonal pressures to take drugs, and to do so effectively they must practice such resistance under simulated conditions and receive reinforcement and support for such behaviors. These programs often use behavioral rehearsal and role-playing exercises conducted by same-age or older peer group leaders who have high credibility or respect among those in the target group. Peer leaders also serve as effective role models who do not use drugs.

TABLE 3.1 Exemplary Substance Use Prevention Outcome Studies

Study	Sample Size/ Grade Level	Target Drug(s)	Emphasis of Intervention	Significant Findings	Follow-Up (months)
Botvin, Baker, Dusenbury, Botvin, & Diaz (1995)	3,597/ Grades 5-6	tobacco, alcohol, marijuana	life skills training	reduced use for all target drugs	36
Dielman, Shope, Leech, & Butchart (1989)	1,505/ Grade 7	alcohol	resistance training	students with prior use show less alcohol use and misuse	26
Elder et al. (1993)	2,668/ Grades 7-8	tobacco	resistance training	reduced tobacco use	none
Flynn et al. (1994)	5,458/ Grades 4-6	tobacco	resistance training; resistance training + mass media	resistance training + mass media more effective than resistance training alone on cigarette smoking	24
Hansen & Graham (1991)	2,135/ Grade 7	alcohol, tobacco, marijuana	resistance training; social norms; resistance training + social norms; information only	social norms and resistance training + social norms each more effective than resistance training alone or information only for all target drugs	none
Johnson et al. (1990)	1,607/ Grades 6-7	tobacco, alcohol, marijuana	comprehensive: school program + parent involvement + community activities + mass media	reduced cigarette and marijuana use	36

The Life Skills Training (LST) Program developed by Botvin and his colleagues (Dusenbury, Botvin, & James-Ortiz, 1990) has a slightly different philosophy and orientation. LST rests on the premise that multiple personal and social factors can account for drug use. For example, students might take drugs because of low self-esteem, anxiety, inability to resist peer pressure, poor communication skills, or an inability to set effective personal plans and goals. In LST, each of these areas is targeted for training. Skills are developed through a social learning training sequence that consists of a recurring loop of procedures involving definition of the target skill, effective modeling of the skill by others, and trainees' practice of the new skills followed by immediate feedback on skill performance. Homework assignments are often used to increase skill mastery.

Environment-Oriented Programs

In terms of programs with a broad environmental focus, Flynn et al. (1994) have demonstrated that an intensive, well-orchestrated mass media effort offered in conjunction with a school-based program can be effective. Other media programs have also been successful (Kaufman, Jason, Sawlski, & Halpert, 1994).

The Midwestern Prevention Project (MPP) developed by Pentz and her colleagues (Johnson et al., 1990) is commonly cited as an effective model for community-wide interventions. MPP begins when students are in junior high school and continues through the high school years and has operated in multiple schools in two large midwestern metropolitan areas. The program contains five coordinated components: a school intervention that trains students in peer resistance skills, a parent component, community organization activities involving multiple agencies, involvement of local health policy makers, and a mass media campaign. The parent component includes parents' participation with children in related homework assignments, as well as parent training in drug prevention activities and communication skills. MPP targets several health behaviors and has also been successful in modifying children's nutritional intake and physical activity levels.

Finally, the effort of O'Donnell, Hawkins, Catalano, Abbott, and Day (1995) deserves notice as an intervention directed at multiple problems, including drug use, school failure, and behavioral problems. Because these negative outcomes share several common risk factors, O'Donnell et al. developed a program to modify these factors simultaneously. The intervention, which extends from first to sixth grade, includes teacher training in proactive management procedures (see Chapter 4), new learning approaches in the classroom, social skills training for children, and parent education. Outcome data suggest this extended intervention increases children's attachment and commitment to school, improves school performance, and reduces drug use and early signs of delinquent activity.

Most impressive is the magnitude of change achieved in various psychosocial investigations. For instance, some outcome differences obtained between experimental and comparison groups in the studies from

Table 3.1 reflect a 37% difference in the prevalence of tobacco use (Elder et al., 1993); a 33% reduction in the onset of smoking (Flynn et al., 1994); 19% and 38% reductions in the respective numbers of youth who smoked or used marijuana in the past month (Johnson et al., 1990); 45% and 87% reductions in the rate of monthly alcohol use and the onset of problems associated with alcohol, respectively (Hansen & Graham, 1991); and, finally, a reduction in the odds of smoking, drinking immoderately, or using marijuana of up to 40% (Botvin, Baker, Dusenbury, Botvin, & Diaz, 1995). These data reflect that the most successful programs have been able to produce socially meaningful changes in drug behaviors.

In their attempt to refine programs, preventionists have explored a number of issues, such as the timing and duration of intervention, the value of booster sessions, and the generality of program effects across target populations and settings. Other issues involve who can be effective in conducting the program and assessment of program factors contributing to obtained outcomes. These matters are briefly discussed below.

Timing and target drugs. Most children experiment first with cigarettes and alcohol, and then marijuana, before moving on to other drugs such as barbiturates, cocaine, or hallucinogens. Therefore, the former three substances are labeled as *gateway* drugs and are the target of most programs, although some programs target only one of these, usually tobacco or alcohol.

Most interventions begin when students are in late elementary or junior high school (Grades 5-8), because this is the period when students first try drugs. The best time point for intervention has not been determined and probably varies across target groups and types of drugs, but early intervention is important because delaying the age at which youth use drugs has preventive implications. Early onset of drug taking is one risk factor for later use and misuse (Johnson et al., 1990).

Duration and booster sessions. Short-term interventions achieve, at best, short-term results. Community-oriented programs have continued for several years (Flynn et al., 1994; Johnson et al., 1990; O'Donnell et al., 1995). Although many classroom-based interventions are not lengthy, consisting of 30 or fewer sessions, it seems critical either to spread out the basic program over successive school years or to provide booster or follow-up contact of some sort after the initial program has ended. This appears particularly important for the maintenance of program impact during follow-up. Few programs without boosters have achieved long-term results.

Program generality. Many different types of change agents have successfully conducted drug programs, including research staff, college students, teachers, and peers. Older peers seem particularly effective. Programs have been successful with diverse elementary, junior high, and high school populations, and some interventions have also been crafted for specific ethnic groups (Botvin, Schinke, Epstein, & Diaz, 1994). The scope of some programs has varied from a single school to multisite implementations conducted in different states.

Effective program components. Contemporary programs are multidimensional interventions that contain many features, making it impossible to specify which factors are most responsible for program success (Hansen, 1992). In addition to the factors already mentioned, interventions also contain a mixture of other elements, such as information, social support, establishment of conservative norms related to drug use, and modification of erroneous beliefs and stereotypes concerning the prevalence and acceptability of drugs. Several of the studies listed in Table 3.1 are beginning to evaluate the differential impact of some of these components, but it is too early to reach any conclusions.

Gap between research and practice. As research evidence continues to surface regarding what types of drug programs are most effective, the challenge will be to convince schools to replace their existing programs with interventions that have been empirically validated. General issues related to effective program diffusion are discussed in Chapter 6.

SUMMARY

Overall, current research on drug programs offers some of the strongest support for the effectiveness of school-based prevention. Prevention is possible in terms of delaying the onset of drug use and reducing the number of children who take drugs and the quantity of drugs they consume. Results do endure over time, have practical significance, and are relevant for diverse school populations.

The most successful projects target psychosocial factors. Programs train children systematically in the skills they need to understand and resist pressures to take drugs, parents and peers are involved in the intervention, intensive mass media campaigns are developed, and communitywide programs are connected to school-based efforts. Booster or follow-up sessions appear essential for classroom-based programs to ensure that short-terms gains are maintained over time.

4

PREVENTION OF
ACADEMIC PROBLEMS

Given that the primary mission of schools is academic instruction, it is important to discuss the prevention of learning problems.

EXTENT OF THE PROBLEM

Lack of success in school takes many forms and affects many students. For example, up to 18% of U.S. high school seniors read at least 4 years below grade level (Dryfoos, 1990). Approximately 13% of 17-year-olds may be functionally illiterate; one half of 13-year-olds do not have a good grasp of elemental scientific concepts; among high school seniors, nearly 40% lack the ability to draw logical inferences from written material, 20% cannot write a persuasive essay, and 33% cannot correctly solve multistep mathematical problems (Murphy, 1990). Up to one fifth of all students are retained in grade at least once at some time in their school careers (Meisels & Liaw, 1993), and, on average, 25% of students drop out of high school (National Center for Education Statistics, 1986).

WHO IS AT RISK?

The problems enumerated above tend to be more prevalent as a function of certain familial and school characteristics, such as minority status, socioeconomic level, and school location. Inner-city schools tend to have student bodies that function at lower levels of academic achievement and to have lower graduation rates than other schools. Minority youth tend to do more poorly than whites on many indices of academic performance. Up to 40% of minority youth may be functionally illiterate (Murphy,

1990), and minority dropout rates in some urban inner-city areas exceed 50% (Cairns, Cairns, & Neckerman, 1989; Ensminger & Slusarick, 1992).

Particular risk indices vary in their importance over the course of schooling. The best single predictor of academic performance before a child reaches elementary school is the family's socioeconomic level, with many more children from the lowest income levels doing poorly. Once in elementary school, however, academic performance becomes a better predictor of subsequent performance. Retention in grade at any time between kindergarten and eighth grade is associated with later poor academic and personal/social outcomes regardless of a child's gender, race, or socioeconomic status (Meisels & Liaw, 1993). The presence of early academic problems predicts not only later learning problems but also subsequent behavioral and social difficulties, special education placement, and dropping out of school. Although not all pupils display the same developmental sequence, the progression of serious academic problems often proceeds through a four-stage sequence: from early academic problems, to grade retention, to special education placement, to dropping out of school or graduation with low levels of academic achievement.

At the same time, academic problems are not the only important risk factor. Early behavior problems in school, particularly aggressive behavior and poor peer relations, also predict later academic and behavioral difficulties (Cairns et al., 1989); only 30% of children with serious behavior problems function at or above grade level (Knitzer, Steinberg, & Fleisch, 1990).

In summary, several academic indicators are important bellwethers of school failure. Prevention programs that can modify levels of academic achievement, grade retention, special educational placement, and dropout rates are likely to have meaningful impacts on children's school careers. This chapter focuses on interventions that have emphasized these outcomes.

IMPORTANCE OF
EARLY INTERVENTION

As a general rule, children do not outgrow their learning problems. Once children begin falling behind their peers academically, the overwhelming majority will fall further behind over time and will be unable to catch up through regular avenues of instruction. The longer academic problems are ignored, the greater the need for intensive and sustained intervention, which many public schools are unequipped to provide.

As a result, many educators now agree that the prevention of learning problems depends on early intervention, and a growing body of research suggests that prevention should occur before children at highest risk reach elementary school. As noted above, the children at highest academic risk are those from low-income households. Many early childhood interventions have targeted this group for intervention; these programs are discussed in the following section.

EARLY CHILDHOOD PROGRAMS

Early childhood programs include programs for infants, toddlers, and preschoolers. The ultimate academic intent of these programs is to promote children's readiness for school. *School readiness* is a general term that refers to the adequate maturation of linguistic, cognitive, and social competencies that help a child meet the demands of formal academic instruction beginning in first grade. For a variety of reasons, it is believed that children from low-income households do not receive sufficient stimulation and socialization experiences to develop these developmental competencies. Therefore, the thrust of most early childhood programs is to work with both children and their caregivers to prepare children for formal schooling.

There is not much disagreement about the immediate effects of early childhood programs; many programs have had significant short-term positive impacts (Casto & White, 1985). The major concern involves whether the effects of these programs are durable. Initially, it was believed that most effects from early childhood programs faded over time; now it is known that high-quality early childhood programs can produce long-term benefits, although all the factors that lead to more lasting changes are unclear.

For example, three reviewers have examined the long-term preventive effects of early education programs. Lazar and Darlington (1982) have summarized findings from the Consortium for Longitudinal Studies, a project consisting of 11 independent research groups who agreed to pool their follow-up data for a collaborative study. These early intervention programs represent a variety of center-based and home-based interventions for infants and preschoolers. The programs varied in duration from 1 to 4 years, and follow-ups ranged from 5 to 13 years. Barnett (1990) has summarized information from six additional large-scale, public preschool programs, with follow-up periods ranging from 3 to 12 years.

long-term impacts are greater

Data presented by Lazar and Darlington (1982) and Barnett (1990) indicate significant long-term effects for early intervention on special education placement, grade retention, and school dropout rate. Across the 17 programs evaluated, 48.5% fewer experimental children were eventually placed in special education classes, 32% fewer were retained in grade, and there were 26% fewer dropouts. These data reflect meaningful long-term impacts on children's school functioning.

The researchers' findings on levels of school achievement are less straightforward. Results aggregated across the independent research projects (Lazar & Darlington, 1982) suggest that experimental children did significantly better than controls on math but not on reading. Barnett (1990) concludes that early childhood public programs did not result in significantly better school achievement, but also indicates that the procedures used to collect test scores from children probably did not provide an adequate test of this effect. Follow-up data were inconsistently collected, attrition during testing was high, and nonstandardized instruments were often used to measure achievement.

A somewhat different approach to evaluating early childhood programs has been taken by Slavin and his colleagues (Slavin, Karweit, & Madden, 1989; Slavin, Karweit, & Wasik, 1994). Using a "best-evidence synthesis" approach, these reviewers examined hundreds of interventions for students at risk for learning problems, searching for programs that assessed at the very least reading achievement during early elementary school using standardized measures. Moreover, they selected only studies that possessed good internal and external validity. For example, among other criteria, selected studies used equivalent comparison groups (many used random assignment to conditions), gave signs of being well implemented, and sufficiently described their procedures and materials so that the programs could be replicated by others.

Slavin et al. (1994) evaluated several programs not reviewed by Lazar and Darlington (1982) and Barnett (1990), such as the Milwaukee Project, the Carolina Abecedarian Project, the Family Development Research Program, and the Parent-Child Development Center Model. Slavin et al. (1994) also conclude that early childhood intervention is effective in preparing at-risk children for school; they indicate that the more successful programs they evaluated were multicomponent interventions of comparatively longer duration and involved intensive participation by both children and parents. It appears particularly important to either continue the intervention for several years or in some way offer follow-up or booster services to families up until the time the children enter elementary school. To give the reader a flavor of the elements that make up successful early intervention programs, I describe two below.

The Perry Preschool Program (Schweinhart & Weikart, 1988), which was part of the Consortium for Longitudinal Studies, has probably become the most frequently cited and discussed early childhood program because of its dramatic long-term results. Children from low-income families participated in an intensive 2-year preschool program when they were ages 3 and 4. Teachers were carefully trained and supervised, the teacher-pupil ratio was kept low (between 1:5 and 1:6), and the curriculum emphasized child-initiated learning. Staff also involved parents in program activities, conducted home visits to help parents further their children's social and cognitive development, and attended to the non-educational needs of families by helping them secure needed child care, medical, and social services.

Long-term results were noticeable up to 14 years after the program ended. During their subsequent school careers, the experimental children earned higher grades, failed less frequently, spent fewer years in special education, and graduated from high school at a higher rate than did control students. At age 19, there were also significant differences between experimental and control students on several social and vocational indicators. Experimental students were less likely to have ever been arrested (31% vs. 51%) or to be on welfare (18% vs. 32%), and more likely to be employed (50% vs. 32%) and pursuing continuing education (38% vs. 21%).

Findings from the Carolina Abecedarian Project (Horacek, Ramey, Campbell, Hoffmann, & Fletcher, 1987) illustrate the importance of program timing and intensity on outcomes. Children from low-income households were selected for program participation based on their status on a composite risk index assessing, among other things, parental educational levels, absence of extended family who might provide support, welfare status, and family members' IQ levels. The typical family was African American and headed by an unmarried young (mean age = 19) female who had not completed high school. Four successive cohorts of approximately 30 children each were matched on risk and randomly assigned to intervention or control conditions. The duration and intensity of the intervention varied among three experimental cohorts: some received a preschool intervention only, some a school-age intervention only, and some both components. The intensive preschool experiences began in early infancy and lasted 6 to 8 hours a day, 5 days a week, for 50 weeks until the child entered kindergarten. The school-age intervention involved the activities of a special resource teacher who visited the home during Grades K through 2 and taught parents how to help the child in reading, math, and other educational activities.

In general, a linear relationship was found between success in school and the timing and intensity of the intervention. For instance, the percentage of children who were retained in at least one grade was 50% for the controls, 38% for those receiving the later-occurring school intervention, 29% for those receiving the extended and early preschool program, and only 16% for those receiving the full preschool and school-age interventions. Similar findings resulted when children's standardized achievement test scores were analyzed. Furthermore, the school performance of children receiving the full program did not differ significantly from the performance of a randomly selected affluent, white, middle-class comparison group. Horacek et al. (1987) conclude that their findings "demonstrate the importance of identifying high-risk children early in life and the effectiveness of educational intervention to improve school performance" (p. 762).

In contrast to the most successful early intervention programs, Slavin et al. (1994) indicate that more limited interventions produce much more limited results. For example, 1-year preschool programs and full-day kindergarten programs yield substantial benefits in the short term, but their impacts usually dissipate over time. Extra-year kindergarten and transitional first-grade programs are other types of interventions that have been used for children who are not ready for the academic demands of regular first grade. Students retained in kindergarten or first grade do profit academically from retention, but these gains wash out when the children subsequently receive regular classroom instruction. As a result, such children never really catch up to their peers academically.

In summary, data from different types of programs using different evaluative strategies and follow-up periods converge to suggest that early childhood interventions can have important long-term effects on school adjustment for populations at greatest risk for subsequent school problems, namely, children from low-income households. It is possible to prepare these at-risk children in such a way that they are able to profit from regular school instruction, but early intervention must be begun before first grade and must be sustained.

Unfortunately, it is not possible to disentangle the most effective elements of multicomponent early childhood interventions. Most programs provide a range of services concurrently to children and their families. For example, children's development is stimulated during play and more structured cognitive programs. At the same time, their caregivers are given social support as well as specific training in child rearing and child development, and are generally empowered to secure necessary medical, social, vocational, and educational services for themselves and their children. In fact, many researchers of early intervention programs adopt an ecological stance in interpreting outcome findings (Brooks-Gunn, McCormick, Shapiro, Benasich, & Black, 1994). It is believed that children ultimately benefit because their primary caretakers become better socializers and educators who support and nurture their children's growth and development. Nevertheless, so many different elements characterize early childhood programs that it is not possible to specify which program features account for which effects.

Conclusions regarding the success of early intervention apply only to low-income children, and it is important to develop more accurate predictors of future learning problems. Not all children from low-income households experience school failure, and some children from higher socioeconomic classes also have later learning problems. Thus we need more effective methods of identifying different groups of children at risk for later academic problems.

INTERVENTIONS AT THE ELEMENTARY LEVEL

Slavin et al. (1994) also evaluated primary prevention programs that offer immediate help to first-grade children to prevent the occurrence of serious learning problems. Tutoring programs appear to constitute a particularly effective preventive strategy. Findings from 16 studies evaluating five different tutoring programs yielded a high mean effect size of 0.89. These programs involved one-on-one reading tutoring of first-grade children conducted by adults (teachers, aides, or parent volunteers). Although there was some reduction in effect at follow-ups ranging from 9 to 12 months later (mean ES = 0.58 from four studies), the findings at follow-up are equal to or surpass the immediate posttreatment effects obtained from many other elementary-level intervention programs. The success of adult tutoring programs led Slavin et al. (1994) to conclude, "One-on-one tutoring of low-achieving primary grade students is without doubt one of the most effective instructional innovations available" (p. 167).

Other researchers have independently come to positive conclusions about the value of tutoring. For example, peer tutoring is also effective.

Peer tutoring appears more helpful for math (mean posttreatment ES of 0.60) than for reading (0.29), according to a review of 65 studies by Cohen, Kulik, and Kulik (1982). An additional benefit of peer tutoring is that the tutors also benefit from the process, in that they show improved academic functioning (mean ES for tutors = 0.62 in math and 0.21 in reading).

Greenwood, Delquadri, and Hall (1989) have summarized positive findings from seven studies assessing another tutoring program called Classwide Peer Tutoring (CWPT). In an eighth, large-scale, carefully executed 4-year study, Greenwood et al. (1989) report that CWPT was effective in significantly improving the standardized test performance of low-income children in reading (mean ES = 0.57), mathematics (mean ES = 0.37), and language (mean ES = 0.60). Moreover, the final fourth-grade performance of experimental children did not differ significantly from high-SES children who were not initially at risk for school problems and received regular classroom instruction. This is one of the few investigations (see Horacek et al., 1987, described earlier) that has indicated that the later performance of both at-risk and not-at-risk children does not significantly differ.

Apart from tutoring, the only clearly successful primary prevention program identified by Slavin et al. (1994) is Success For All, which was developed by Slavin's own research group. Although one might wonder about the authors' promotion of their own program, current findings for Success For All meet the tests of an effective intervention. Success For All is a multicomponent, comprehensive, schoolwide program that combines preschool and kindergarten programs with one-on-one tutoring in the early elementary grades plus family support activities and other services. As a comprehensive program, Success For All bridges the gap between primary and secondary prevention efforts. The idea is to prevent academic problems before first grade through intensive, high-quality preschool and kindergarten programs (primary prevention), to tutor first graders who have early reading problems, and to continue tutoring and offering other academic services until children's academic achievement is at grade level (secondary prevention).

The Success For All program began in 1986 in Baltimore and has since expanded to schools in 12 states. As is true with any large-scale, multisite intervention, the program varies somewhat from site to site, depending on local resources and needs. The prototypical first-grade program places from 2 to 6 tutors in each classroom to provide individual 20-minute daily tutoring sessions to each child and to assist the regular classroom teacher in small-group reading instruction using principles of cooperative learning. Children are grouped according to reading performance levels within Grades 1 to 3, but formal reading instruction begins in the second semester of kindergarten. There is a half-day preschool and/or a full-day kindergarten using a curriculum emphasizing language development and balancing academic readiness activities with nonacademic music, art, and social activities. Family support teams also work in each school to involve parents actively in the education of their children. These support teams offer parent education and stress the importance of such topics as proper sleep and nutrition, eye and hearing tests, and regular school attendance.

Outcome data from Success For All on reading achievement combined across 43 cohorts of children from Grades 1 through 3 in eight schools in four cities indicate strong effects (mean ES = 0.49), and these results are almost twice as high as those in the lowest quartile of initial achievement (mean ES = 0.87). These latter data suggest the program has been most helpful for children at greatest risk. Experimental schools have served diverse student populations, including Cambodian children with limited English proficiency and children from rural communities and inner-city neighborhoods.

Data on special education placements have been obtained only in the Baltimore schools; these have favored program children, with a 50% reduction in special education placement through the end of Grade 3. A final indication of program impact is that for all 43 cohorts, only 3.9% and 12% of program children, respectively, have been found to be performing 2 or more years behind grade level or to be 1 year behind. In contrast, the corresponding proportions for controls are 11.7% and 26.5%.

The findings from Success For All are impressive. The major reservation involves the feasibility of program implementation on a wide scale. As more schools become interested in this intervention, it will be important to monitor how well the entire set of preschool, kindergarten, and early primary-grade programs for at-risk students can be implemented in different settings and what happens if only parts of the program are enacted. Some data currently indicate that program effects for Success For All increase over the first 4 years of program operation, suggesting that proficiency in program practices takes considerable time to acquire. Moreover, it is not known which elements of this complex, comprehensive effort are responsible for the changes obtained to date.

In summary, there is evidence that the primary prevention of learning problems is possible through several vehicles. Intervention before first grade is essential for children at highest risk—that is, those from low-

TABLE 4.1 Mean Effect Sizes for Effective Secondary Prevention
Academic Programs

Type of Program	Effect Size
Classroom-Based Programs	
continuous progress programs ($n = 11$)	0.43
individualized instruction ($n = 1$)	0.57
cooperative learning ($n = 2$)	0.45
Pullout Programs	
typical Chapter 1 program ($n = 1$)	0.25 (reading)
	0.12 (math)
remedial tutoring programs ($n = 3$)	0.69
computer-assisted instruction ($n = 4$)	0.34

SOURCE: Data are drawn from Slavin et al. (1989).

income households—and has been achieved by several early intervention
programs serving both children and parents. In elementary school, various
forms of tutoring programs and one comprehensive program, Success For
All, currently seem the most successful.

SECONDARY PREVENTION
OF LEARNING PROBLEMS

The distinction between primary and secondary prevention programs is
sometimes difficult to make. Strictly speaking, secondary prevention
programs intervene after a child has demonstrated learning problems but
soon enough so that these difficulties are not long standing.

Table 4.1 lists the outcomes for the successful secondary prevention
programs identified by Slavin et al. (1989). Some of the terminology used
to describe these programs may seem foreign to the reader. Basically,
Slavin et al. note three commonalities among the in-classroom programs:
continuous progress, individualized instruction, and cooperative learning.
These programs share the following characteristics: (a) maximum time
allotted to direct instruction and learning; (b) frequent monitoring of
student progress, with opportunities for practice to achieve mastery; and
(c) a structured hierarchy of learning tasks matched to students' ability
level. The main distinctions among the programs are that cooperative
learning involves students of mixed ability working together to learn and

receiving reinforcement based on the learning of all team members. Individualized instruction involves student work on programmed or carefully sequenced materials, with individual teacher-student contact. Continuous programs are a form of mastery-based learning in which students proceed through a hierarchy of skills; instruction occurs through a variety of mechanisms, but most instruction is provided by teachers to groups of students, who may be grouped or regrouped according to their levels of skills in different subjects.

Pullout programs are interventions offered to children outside the regular classroom but short of special education placements. Tutoring and computer-aided instruction are self-explanatory. Chapter 1 programs are programs that involve out-of-classroom individualized instruction given to low-income students who have demonstrated learning problems. It is the most common form of assistance provided to low-income students in the public schools; 84% of all reading help and 76% of all mathematics aid occurs in this format. Unfortunately, Slavin et al. (1989) could calculate an effect size for only one such program, which was quite modest in impact (0.25 in reading and 0.12 in math), and they found only two other Chapter 1 programs that seemed to be effective. Other authors using different criteria have come to the conclusion that the typical forms of remediation provided to high-risk public school children are insufficient to correct their learning problems (Archambault, 1989; Rowan & Guthrie, 1989). These interventions are neither intensive nor extensive enough to help children make up lost academic ground.

Naming or describing each of the intervention programs found successful by Slavin et al. (1989, 1994) will not help identify these programs for many readers. Few reports of the interventions deemed successful have been published. Slavin et al. (1989, 1994) sorted through more than 700 unpublished reports of educational programs available through the U.S. Department of Education to locate the two dozen or so programs highlighted in their texts. The difficulty in obtaining information about programs that have been carefully evaluated has implications for the diffusion of successful interventions; this topic is discussed in Chapter 6.

Characteristics of Effective Programs

Despite variety in materials and curricula across programs, the patterning and character of instructional processes are highly similar across many elementary-level primary and secondary prevention academic interventions. These programs tend to emphasize the following principles:

(a) Allot as much time to academic instruction as possible, (b) provide extra assistance at the first sign of difficulty with new material, (c) present material at a brisk pace that challenges students but also provides sufficient opportunities for success, (d) monitor student progress carefully and reinforce students for both effort and product, and (e) be sure that instruction is intensive enough and of sufficient duration to ensure mastery of basic skills. In other words, many of the same principles identified as effective for teaching basic skills for all students (Brophy, 1986) apply equally well to students at academic risk.

CLASSROOM AND SCHOOL FACTORS

Although specific interventions are important, preventive programs cannot be divorced from their ecological contexts. Programs are implemented in classrooms and schools; these important levels of analysis are discussed below.

Proactive Classroom Management

Traditionally, classroom management techniques have focused on control and discipline to reduce existing levels of undesirable student behavior. Another perspective has more recently emerged, however, that has clear implications for prevention: proactive classroom management (PCM). PCM emphasizes the creation and maintenance of a learning environment that simultaneously prevents behavioral problems from occurring and actively promotes high levels of achievement. Gettinger (1988) has synthesized PCM's three general features: (a) It is preventive in character, requiring the teacher to have a plan in mind and to act in advance to anticipate and prepare for various eventualities; (b) it recognizes the inseparability of students' behavior from their learning activities; and (c) it emphasizes management of the entire group or class of students, rather than individuals.

In brief, teachers effective in classroom management know how to establish a clear routine for running the classroom that delineates student responsibilities and teacher expectations regarding academic and social behavior. Students know what is expected, how teachers will monitor their activities, and what the consequences of poor or good performance will be. Furthermore, teachers are adept at moment-to-moment monitoring of group behavior; they can anticipate problems and promptly cue students toward appropriate behavior before disorder results. Finally, teachers are adept at pacing; they know when to introduce new material, when to review current work, and when to ask for repetition of previously learned material to ensure mastery.

PCM has promise as a preventive strategy. Teachers can successfully learn PCM practices, and their subsequent introduction into the classroom has been shown to result in significantly less student misbehavior and significantly more on-task behavior (Evertson, 1985; Evertson, Emmer, Sanford, & Clements, 1983). PCM has also served as one component in other preventive interventions (Hawkins, Von Cleve, & Catalano, 1991).

School Factors

Evidence suggests that schools affect students beyond what could be expected from classroom teaching practices and the ability levels and characteristics of students. In fact, substantial differences in outcomes have been noted across schools, school effects are fairly consistent and durable over time, and schools that are successful in one domain also tend to be effective in others (Good & Weinstein, 1986; Purkey & Smith, 1983; Rutter, 1983). Although there is a need to clarify the exact factors that make schools effective, there is general agreement that the following are important: (a) a clear emphasis on academics and a system to encourage and reward students' accomplishments; (b) a shared sense of purpose and a value system that emphasizes high academic standards, collaboration among staff, and positive relationships between teachers and students; (c) a supportive administrative structure and strong leadership; and (d) clear procedures for monitoring and modifying programs and policies.

The implication of these findings is that the general culture and organization of many schools can be improved, which in turn can result in better student outcomes. Organizational changes in schools constitute a long, complex undertaking, however, and it is unclear how this process should be initiated (Sarason, 1971). Although there is much still to be learned about changing schools, two successful projects illustrate the benefits that can achieved by such efforts.

The Yale-New Haven Project (Comer, 1985) is an effort at wide-scale systems-level changes in the norms and operations of an entire elementary school. Teachers, administrators, parents, and community-based mental health professionals collaborate to govern the school, establish policies and programs, monitor curricula and new services, and enhance staff development. Parents, in particular, assume substantial responsibility in school activities and on school committees. The overall intent is to develop a positive school climate that promotes and integrates the educational, recreational, and social development of students. This project began in 1968 in two inner-city schools with historically low levels of student achievement and high rates of behavior and attendance problems. The latter have virtually vanished from the program schools, and the schools have risen from the bottom to the top of city rankings in terms of academic achievement. A 3-year follow-up indicated that program students were performing at grade level in academic subjects and were 2 years ahead of controls; program students also reported more competence at school and overall. The Yale-New Haven Project has received national attention and is currently being replicated in other school districts.

A second successful attempt at organizational change has been reported by Gottfredson (1987). A neighborhood school serving students from primarily low-income black families was modified in several ways. Administrators, teachers, and research staff collaborated in the planning and monitoring of efforts at schoolwide change to encourage student responsibility, provide consistent rewards for student performance, and increase social support for students. Cooperative learning strategies were also introduced into the classroom, parents become more involved in school activities, and extracurricular community-based activities were developed. Although academic outcomes were not assessed, the 2-year program significantly improved teacher morale, increased students' sense of integration and attachment to school, and reduced student disruptive behavior.

In summary, environmental characteristics of the classroom and school are also important influences on academic achievement. It is reasonable to believe that teachers who effectively implement new preventive curricula are also skilled in PCM, and that schools deemed generally effective most likely produce better results when they initiate new programs. These assumptions need to be verified empirically, however. Further discussion of how features of the school environment affect behavior can be found in Moos (1979) and Toro et al. (1985).

SUMMARY

For children from low-income families, primary prevention should occur before the first grade. Delaying intervention until these children demonstrate learning problems in elementary school often guarantees the status quo: Large numbers of children will experience early school failure that will intensify over time. Most schools do not provide the necessary services to children at academic risk; the help that is offered produces too little impact and is too late in coming.

There is increasing evidence that early intervention produces long-term benefits when multicomponent, intensive, long-term intervention involves both children and parents. The successful elements of different programs have yet to be identified, but most programs have combined family support with early childhood educational programs.

The best single predictor of future academic performance is early academic performance. This is usually true regardless of a child's social status, gender, or race. Therefore, prompt intervention in the early grades for children with learning difficulties appears critical to the prevention of later problems. Several prevention-oriented academic programs have been carefully evaluated and can be replicated in other settings. Individualized and continuous learning curriculum approaches, cooperative learning, computer-assisted instruction, tutoring, and comprehensive efforts such as Success For All have demonstrated their promise in producing significant and meaningful impacts on children's achievement that have holding power over time.

The value of programs to prevent academic problems should not be underestimated, either in terms of the extent of learning difficulties experienced by many children or in terms of the spillover effects that may occur. For instance, some early intervention programs that have been successful in preventing academic problems have also been effective in preventing behavioral forms of school maladjustment (Johnson, 1988; Schweinhart & Weikart, 1988). Other researchers have noted that additional unanticipated, long-term benefits of early intervention programs have included significant reductions in chronic delinquency (e.g., Yoshikawa, 1994). Thus, some early intervention programs have produced substantial benefits that radiate beyond the academic realm.

Preventionists have historically neglected the academic needs of target populations. This neglect appears to be changing slowly, however. Several researchers working with students at academic risk have independently come to the judgment that academic components should be added to psychosocial interventions designed to prevent behavioral dysfunction (Coie & Krehbiel, 1984; Cowen, Hightower, Pedro-Carroll, & Work, 1990; Hawkins et al., 1991; Jason et al., 1992). Because these interventions have produced positive results, future research should see more programs that address the academic needs of target groups.

5

HEALTH EDUCATION

Initial efforts at health education in the early 1900s provided children with basic information about communicable disease and the importance of basic medical care and attention. Health education has now evolved toward activities designed to modify health-related behavior (Allensworth, 1993). Moreover, the concept of health has expanded to include not only physical but mental, emotional, and social dimensions (Perry, 1984), so that virtually everything can be viewed in one way or another as falling under the purview of health education. One way to subdivide the broad field of health education is to consider the two major categories of preventable physical health problems of schoolchildren related to (a) injuries and physical violence and (b) emerging habits and lifestyles that affect health. This chapter focuses only on the latter category, addressing studies directed at changing children's eating patterns and physical activity levels and influencing their sexual behavior. Smoking and drug use, which also have implications for health, are treated in Chapter 3.

NEED AND RATIONALE
FOR HEALTH EDUCATION

Resnicow et al. (1992) summarize data suggesting the need for physical health education. Depending on the criteria and methodology used, up to 30% of children have elevated total cholesterol levels, 5% have hypertension, 15% are obese, 60% do not get adequate exercise, and approximately one fifth of high school seniors are regular smokers. In fact, up to 60% of children have at least one risk factor for coronary heart disease by age 12. Many of the factors that place children at risk for later serious health problems are the results of lifestyle choices or behaviors that can be modified. Waiting until adulthood, however, probably reduces the chances of successful intervention, because many established health-related behaviors—such as nutritional intake, diet and exercise patterns, smoking, and drinking—are difficult to change, particularly over the long term (Kaplan, 1984). Therefore, school-based physical health promotion programs have focused on young children who are just developing an understanding of health and behavior, forming attitudes and behaviors related to health and prevention, and becoming able to make decisions and take actions in the pursuit of health.

IMPACT OF HEALTH EDUCATION

Although health education is not new in the schools, carefully conducted outcome studies on its impact did not begin appearing with any frequency until the 1970s (Cortese, 1993). Research on health education has progressed rapidly, however. Reviewers consider current work to be the fourth generation of research and note that the breadth and rigor of research has improved substantially with each new wave of studies (McKinlay, Stone, & Zucker, 1989). Two large-scale evaluations that are particularly impressive in their scope and historical significance are discussed first below, and then other representative programs are briefly reviewed.

School Health Education Evaluation

The School Health Education Evaluation (SHEE) was a massive undertaking involving more than 30,000 children in Grades 4 through 7 from more than 1,000 classrooms in 20 states (Connell, Turner, & Mason, 1985). Four different programs emphasizing cardiovascular health promotion and risk reduction were evaluated. Results expressed in terms of mean effect sizes indicated the programs were more effective in modifying knowledge (mean ES of 0.65) than in changing behavior (mean ES of 0.27), a common finding in many prevention studies. However, there were four other noteworthy findings. First, students receiving 2 years of a program reported significantly more behavioral change than those receiving only 1 year of intervention. Second, the quality of program implementation was related to program outcomes. For example, full program implementation resulted in 85% greater behavioral gains than average levels of implementation.

Third, different levels of program implementation were required to produce maximum impact for different types of programs. For two of the four health programs evaluated, significant behavioral change was not found unless the programs were implemented for at least 20 hours and parents were involved, as the program model suggested. By plotting hours of instruction by magnitude of change for all programs, Connell et al. (1985) have concluded that stable and maximum program effects were obtained only after 50 classroom hours of instruction. The important implications of these three findings is that evaluators must monitor program implementation, because some outcomes should not be expected unless a program has been conducted well and for a sufficient length of time. Chapter 6 discusses the issue of implementation of various prevention programs in more depth. Fourth and finally, a cost-effectiveness analysis suggested that each of the four programs was worth the expense in terms of its obtained outcomes.

Teenage Health Teaching Modules

The Teenage Health Teaching Modules (THTM) project was another extensive undertaking that evaluated health education, but this time at the junior high and high school levels (Errecart et al., 1991). More than 4,800 students attending 149 schools in seven states participated. In this project, a single program, THTM, offered over one school semester was evaluated. THTM consists of 16 modules focused on such topics as nutrition, smoking, drugs, and personal safety. Results were analyzed separately for junior and senior high school participants and, similar to SHEE, program effects were higher for knowledge (ESs of 0.99 and 0.75) than for health-related practices (ESs of 0.36 and 0.42, respectively, for junior and senior high school students). Changes in specifically targeted health behaviors, however, were significant for senior high school students only. For example, the effect sizes for various behaviors were as follows: consumption of fatty foods, 0.26; percentage of students not smoking in the past month, 0.33; percentage not using illicit drugs, 0.28; and the mean number of alcoholic drinks consumed in the past month, 0.30. Systematic efforts at training teachers had positive effects on both program implementation and student outcomes (Ross, Luepker, Nelson, Saavedra, & Hubbard, 1991).

In summary, both SHEE and THTM had positive behavioral effects upon students' health, but both program evaluations were limited in their reliance on self-report outcome measures and lacked follow-up data. Nevertheless, these large multisite evaluations stand as landmark attempts to document the value of health education; they have created substantial visibility for the field of health education, and have stimulated many other programs and outcome studies.

Several theoretical developments in health education parallel those for drug interventions. For example, early health education programs often emphasized educational or information strategies, but these rarely brought about significant behavioral changes. Investigators then began emphasizing skills training approaches and identified some of the same skills emphasized in drug programs, such as refusal skills, assertiveness, media analysis skills, communication, and self-control procedures. In health education, the targets for these skills relate to resisting media and social influences promoting unhealthy behaviors, the modification of eating and physical activity patterns, and individual goal-setting and self-management strategies. Then the importance of moving beyond the classroom and modifying environmental factors that influence target behaviors has been emphasized. As in drug programs, peer and media influences and parental practices have been stressed (Allensworth, 1993).

Programs that have met with the most general success have been multicomponent interventions that combine classroom-based skills training with environmental change. A few successful programs have focused exclusively on the latter dimension. Some representative programs are discussed below.

Classroom-Based Programs

The Know Your Body (KYB) Program has been the subject of considerable research attention. The two basic features of KYB are a classroom curriculum available for Grades K through 7 and periodic medical screening and feedback to children and parents regarding the children's health status. However, there are other program elements as well, including parent involvement, schoolwide activities, and additional services for high-risk youth. KYB, which is guided by social learning theory, uses a combination of modeling, behavioral rehearsal, goal setting, and reinforcement to change children's health-related behaviors.

Research studies have concentrated on KYB's ability to reduce risk for coronary heart disease by modifying diet, physical activities, and cigarette smoking. Unfortunately, schools have implemented different combinations of KYB elements, so it is unclear which elements are producing which outcomes. Nevertheless, findings from several large-scale, multisite investigations indicate KYB has a positive impact on the health status of diverse school populations. Significant effects have been obtained on total cholesterol levels, blood pressure, consumption of healthier foods, physical fitness, and smoking, although not all studies have achieved all these gains (Resnicow et al., 1992; Resnicow, Cross, & Wynder, 1991). In general, stronger results have been found in intensive, multiyear KYB programs in which teachers have carefully implemented program procedures (Bush et al., 1989; Resnicow et al., 1992).

The Heart Health Program attempts to modify children's consumption of nonnutritious snacks through classroom-based social learning principles, using various environmental components to support behavioral change (Coates et al., 1985). Parents are sent information about Heart Health and are asked to support their children's new eating patterns; a schoolwide media campaign also accompanies the program. Posters and flyers prompting healthy food purchases appear in the cafeteria and near school vending machines, and cafeteria staff are trained to reinforce children's appropriate food choices. Findings from two studies have indicated that Heart Health was associated with significant dietary changes for elementary school children; a third study indicated the program could be successfully modified for African American adolescents attending an inner-city high school (Coates et al., 1985).

Programs Directed at Environmental Change

Two approaches emphasizing environmental change have met with success: parent involvement and organizational change in schools.

Parent involvement. Programs that change parental attitudes and habits are likely to have enduring effects on children's health behaviors. For example, parents are important role models and control the foods available and consumed in the home. Although enlisting parents' involvement can be important, with the exception of the classroom-based programs noted above, researchers have not met with very much success in such efforts. One key to obtaining parental involvement is the acceptability of the intervention. Programs that ask parents to attend meetings at school or in the community have been plagued by low rates of attendance and participation (Perry, Crockett, & Pirie, 1987). This is not surprising, given that survey data indicate these activities are least attractive to parents (Perry et al., 1988).

Perry and her colleagues (Crockett, Mullis, Perry, & Luepker, 1989; Perry et al., 1988) have described an innovative home correspondence program, Home Team (HT), that has secured high rates of parental participation (77% or more). HT is a 5-week correspondence program focusing on nutrition that is taught by the parents to their third-grade children. Weekly activities are completed by the children with their parents, who complete scorecards summarizing these events. HT is coordinated with a school-based monitoring system in which children return the scorecards and receive rewards, depending on which activities are completed. Parents are thus motivated to help their children secure these incentives.

Evaluations indicate that HT is successful in terms of reducing total fat and saturated fats in children's diets and in increasing their consumption of healthy foods (Perry et al., 1988). Most important, concurrent changes occur in parents. Parents' attitudes and knowledge about the importance of diet improves, their health communications with their children increase, they give their children more input into food choices, and healthier foods are found present in the home, based upon home visits and inspections by research staff (Crockett et al., 1989). HT is an economical way to modify eating patterns and costs only $7 per family, including the cost of all incentives, but the program has not been evaluated with low-income families.

Organizational change in schools. Two groups of investigators changed the school environment by modifying the school food service. Ellison, Capper, Goldberg, Witschi, and Stare (1989) worked with the management and food preparers of a boarding high school so that healthier foods were purchased and attractively prepared and presented in the school cafeteria. The program was highly successful. Students reduced their sodium and saturated fat intake by up to 20% and demonstrated a statistically significant decrease in blood pressure. These changes were achieved solely through the modification of the food service; no classroom program accompanied this intervention. Parcel, Simons-Morton, O'Hara, Baranowski, and Wilson (1989) made similar changes in school cafeteria practices and report positive results. This intervention also included classroom and physical activity components, so it is not possible to isolate the effects of the changes in the school food service. Changing cafeteria foods can be a particularly economical and effective way to reach many children. The majority of children eat in their schools' cafeterias, and approximately one third of their daily caloric intake occurs at lunch.

Other attempts to change the school environment have focused on physical education and activity programs. There is a moderate to strong inverse relationship between levels of physical exercise and death from many diseases. Obviously, such a relationship does not imply causality, but the suggestion is that a physically active lifestyle is one component of good health. Most children do not engage in appropriate or recommended levels of physical activity, and the majority of their physical activity takes place outside of school (Sallis et al., 1992), suggesting that schools' physical education programs could be improved. Most physical education classes emphasize games and sports that do not enhance physical fitness, and many children do not participate in daily physical education. Sallis et al.'s (1992) review indicates that modifications of physical education programs to improve physical fitness have been successful. In contrast, classroom-based instruction rarely has produced significant changes in physical activity patterns for elementary or high school students.

METHODOLOGICAL ISSUES

There have been many large-scale, multisite investigations suggesting the applicability of health education across multiple grades and for children from different ethnic and socioeconomic status groups. Nevertheless, more information is needed regarding the timing, duration, and active ingredients of health education interventions (Best, 1989; Resnicow, Cherry, & Cross, 1993). In particular, data are needed to answer three prominent and related questions: Are program effects durable? Are results of practical significance obtained? Are programs cost-effective?

Children's new health behaviors must be periodically reinforced if they are to be maintained. Programs achieving significant effects at follow-up have been in the minority, suggesting the need to lengthen current programs; to provide boosters, as has been done with drug programs; or in some way to establish social support and reinforcement for health-related changes. Environmental programs may provide the means to achieve these ends, but the long-term results of these interventions have not been assessed.

The cost-effectiveness of preventive health programs has not been demonstrated (Kaplan, 1984). This is so in part because it is difficult to evaluate the practical significance of many outcomes. For instance, the desired changes in diet and physical exercise that improve health and in turn significantly reduce morbidity and mortality associated with coronary heart disease and other disorders have not been determined (Kaplan, 1984). Statistical significance does not equate with practical significance, and more basic research is needed to assess which changes in health status reduce or increase risk for various diseases.

SEX AND
AIDS EDUCATION

The preventive implications of sex and AIDS education are fairly obvious. Sexual activity presents the possibility of unwanted pregnancy, acquisition of a fatal disease (AIDS), and exposure to various other sexually transmitted diseases. As a result, preventionists distinguish between safe and unsafe sexual practices, that is, practices that increase or lower the likelihood of risk. For AIDS, risky behaviors include inconsistent use or nonuse of condoms during intercourse, coitus with multiple sexual partners, and coitus with someone who is an intravenous drug user.

Despite the fact that some form of sex education has been present in schools for more than a century and that approximately 85% of all U.S. schools currently offer sex education, there is little controlled research on the behavioral impact of these programs. There is a similar lack of information for AIDS education, which is a much more recent phenomenon, but which is now mandated or recommended by all 50 state departments of education (Kirby et al., 1994).

Kirby et al. (1994) identify only 23 published studies evaluating the behavioral impact of sex or AIDS education in the schools, and they note that methodological limitations in the literature permit only tentative conclusions to be drawn. Programs that have had significant positive effects on behavior have shared several common features: (a) a clear and specific focus on reducing sexual risk-taking behaviors, (b) application of a social learning philosophy to understand how sexual behaviors develop and can be changed, (c) an active skills-oriented focus on increasing safe sexual practices, (d) attention to social and media influences regarding sex, and (e) explicit reinforcement of values and norms against risky sexual behaviors. Kirby et al. also emphasize that there is no evidence that the provision of sex or AIDS education leads to increased rates of sexual intercourse or pregnancy. This information is important, because some groups have opposed sex education in the schools in part because of their stated belief that such instruction will increase rates of sexual activity.

Two controlled studies of AIDS education offered to inner-city Latino and African American adolescents are worthy of note (Jemmott, Jemmott,

& Fong, 1992; Walter & Vaughan, 1993). Despite their brevity, both programs obtained significant differences favoring program participants over comparison groups at 3-month follow-up on such behaviors as condom use, sex with high-risk partners, and sex with fewer partners.

Walter and Vaughan (1993) randomly selected a sample of 23 ninth- and eleventh-grade classrooms to receive a specially prepared AIDS prevention curriculum. An important feature of this study was that the intervention was developed based on the results of an initial needs assessment of the target population that indicated the students did not have accurate information about AIDS, held incorrect beliefs about their level of risk, and needed to learn safe sexual practices. Regular classroom teachers were trained to address these issues in a series of five 1-hour classroom sessions. Jemmott et al. (1992) held a day-long workshop for male students and trained African American adults to implement the program, which was based on social learning principles and involved culturally appropriate media and role-playing exercises.

PREGNANCY PREVENTION

Approximately 1 million teenagers become pregnant every year, most of them unintentionally; these figures include about 19% of all African American women aged 15 to 19, 13% of Latinos, and 8% of whites (Alan Guttmacher Institute, 1994). Adolescent mothers are at risk for chronic educational, occupational, and financial difficulties, and their offspring are also at risk for medical, educational, and behavioral problems. In fact, intergenerational effects are possible, given that the offspring of adolescent mothers are more likely to become pregnant when they reach adolescence (Furstenberg, Brooks-Gunn, & Morgan, 1987). Therefore, the prevention of unwanted teenage pregnancies can have substantial practical significance in the lives of many individuals.

Both the conduct and results of pregnancy prevention programs have been controversial. For example, government policies established through the Adolescent Family Life Act of 1981 emphasized funding only prevention programs fostering sexual abstinence as a primary goal, although data are lacking that such programs are effective. In contrast, many researchers agree that pregnancy prevention goals must consider participants' prior sexual history. Although sexual abstinence (i.e., postponing the onset of sexual intercourse) is a feasible objective for youth who have not yet had sexual intercourse, appropriate contraceptive behavior is a more realistic and attainable goal for nonvirgins, who are unlikely to cease having sexual intercourse (see Miller, Card, Paikoff, & Peterson, 1992).

Many wide-ranging conclusions have been expressed regarding the impacts of pregnancy prevention programs, from statements that such programs do not work (Males, 1993) through statements that there are insufficient data to interpret their effects (White & White, 1991), to conclusions that most programs have not changed participants' sexual behaviors (Brooks-Gunn & Paikoff, 1993).

A review of model programs and evaluations suggests that four principles are shared by the most successful programs (Miller et al., 1992): (a) clear and specific program objectives that are relevant to program participants' prior sexual histories; (b) early intervention that occurs before first intercourse, which, depending on the target group, probably means the preteen years; (c) intensive and comprehensive interventions that include components devoted to accurate information, correcting myths and stereotypes about sexuality and pregnancy, relevant skill building in such areas as decision making and assertiveness, and access to contraceptive and reproductive health services; and, finally, (d) a focus on environmental influences upon sexual behavior relative to peers, family life, and social norms.

One example of a successful approach is a program that included the Self Center, an inner-city adolescent reproductive health clinic offering multiple services to students in a nearby junior high or senior high school (Zabin et al., 1986). Center staff, primarily two nurses and two social workers, offered six categories of services, three in the clinic (group education, individual counseling, and medical services) and three in schools (classroom instruction, after-school small-group discussions, and individual counseling). The 3-year program was successful in two major respects: delaying the onset of coital activity of virgin females and substantially changing pregnancy rates (a reduction of 30% in the program schools vs. a 58% increase in control schools). Moreover, process data indicate the receptivity of students in the program schools to the services provided: 85% of the students took advantage of at least one of the Self Center's activities, and the mean number of student contacts was 10.

SUMMARY

Theories driving health education interventions have expanded to recognize the importance of environmental as well as individual factors in health behavior. Classroom-based skills-training approaches have been used most frequently in attempts to modify individual health practices. Many programs emphasize social learning principles and usually combine modeling, behavioral rehearsal, reinforcement, and self-management techniques. Because health education limited solely to the classroom setting has not been consistently effective, environmental factors are also targeted in more successful programs.

Schoolwide activities emphasizing peer support, media messages, and efforts to involve parents have been used. Although it seems particularly important to include parents in children's health education, the most productive way to do so remains unclear. On a broader environmental level, organizational changes in schools' food services and physical education programs are other promising environmental strategies. Because lifetime changes in children's physical health must occur to prevent disease in adulthood, data are needed on the durability of intervention effects and the most effective means to support long-term behavioral change.

Empirical assessment of the behavioral impact of AIDS education is only beginning, and, despite the long history of sex education in schools, we are also just starting now to learn which programs modify sexual behavior. Programs that teach specific skills related to safe sexual practices are emerging as the most productive interventions. The impact of pregnancy prevention programs is not clear, but several successful programs share some of the same features considered important in other health education efforts. In a fashion similar to drug and physical health education, it seems likely that for maximum effect, classroom-based sex, AIDS, and pregnancy interventions will need to be augmented by attention to environmental influences on behavior.

6

PROGRAM DIFFUSION

In terms of major public health benefits, it does not matter much if research suggests that a program is effective if others will not use that program. This chapter focuses on some of the issues related to program diffusion, or the spread of information about innovations (new programs) and the subsequent actions taken by the recipients of such information.

Program diffusion can be divided into four phases: dissemination, adoption, implementation, and maintenance. In brief, dissemination involves the informing of schools about the existence and operation of new programs; adoption is the phase in which a school decides to try a new program; implementation takes place when the program is actually conducted, and may be done well or poorly; and maintenance is the phase in which the program or a part of it is eventually incorporated into the daily school routine following a trial or demonstration period.

Although consensus exists that careful attention to the process of program diffusion is essential (Best, 1989; Fullan, 1991, 1992; House, 1974; Rogers, 1983; Schinke, Botvin, & Orlandi, 1991; Weissberg, Caplan, & Sivo, 1989), program diffusion has been largely neglected by those who develop and evaluate school programs. As a result, many seemingly effective programs have never been used in the schools; others have been introduced but not properly conducted, seriously compromising their impacts; and some programs have simply faded away or been replaced by others for unknown or vague reasons.

Lack of attention to program diffusion is unfortunate, because many schools are seeking help and advice in learning about existing prevention programs (Bosworth & Cueto, 1994). Currently, there is no effective system through which they may do so. State and federal agencies may provide some written information, but often this material is too incomplete to be of much use for replication purposes (Lavin, 1993; Slavin, Karweit, & Wasik, 1994). Some have advocated an enhanced systematic effort at the federal level to coordinate information about effective programs and to help local communities make more informed choices about alternative programs (e.g., Klein, 1993). This proposal requires sufficient funding for staff committed to program diffusion, however, which may not be forthcoming.

Basically, then, a gap exists between the social scientists who develop and test prevention programs and the many schools that could and would adopt them. Several commercial vendors who are expert at social marketing and promotional strategies have been successful in filling this void. Commercial programs constitute the bulk of programs in many school districts (Bosworth & Cueto, 1994; Lavin, 1993). Indeed, preventionists should learn social marketing principles, because programs must be actively promoted to be used (Fredericksen, Solomon, & Brehony, 1984). Unfortunately, many available commercial programs have little or no scientific basis for their procedures, and even if such data are present, most commercial vendors do not effectively provide for the training and consultation needed to implement the programs correctly (Bosworth & Sailes, 1993).

There has been little systematic research on program diffusion, and distinctions have not always been made among the four phases. Most information comes from case studies, theoretical formulations, and personal experiences. The next section summarizes some of the important features of program diffusion in general; this is followed by a more specific discussion of the implementation phase, which has been the subject of more empirical attention.

FACTORS AFFECTING
PROGRAM DIFFUSION

Characteristics of prevention programs frequently related to initial adoption are program complexity, relative advantage and need, cost, and compatibility. Often these variables are related. For instance, new programs must be perceived as fulfilling unmet needs or as being more advantageous than existing practices. *Complexity* here refers to how easy it is to understand what an innovation actually entails and thus the implications of its adoption. School administrators often emphasize the financial costs of new programs, but teachers tend to view costs in more personal ways, in terms of the time and behavioral demands of trying something new. Finally, programs must be compatible with local norms, values, and beliefs. This suggests that preventionists might have to develop different program formats to suit diverse groups based on age, ethnic diversity, and gender.

Another element often mentioned in relation to program adoption is the interaction between an external agent and an internal advocate or champion (Scheirer, 1990). In other words, someone from outside a school who is in a position to disseminate information and to provide technical resources about a new program teams up with someone from within the school who advocates strongly for program adoption. Personal contact with an external agent is much more effective than written communication; the external agent can provide program details, manuals, and other materials and can serve as a consultant or trainer once the program is adopted. The internal champion within the system knows how the local schools work in terms of where the power lies, who it is important to talk to, how to get decisions made, and so on. For effective program diffusion, the individuals promoting program adoption must attend to the local politics and administration of each school and district.

There is a critical need for data on the discontinuation of innovations. Schools already conduct many preventive programs; as scientific evaluations accumulate to suggest that other programs are probably more effective, the challenge will be to convince schools to discard their current programs. Unfortunately, we do not know very much about what influences educators to cease using a program and replace it with something new. Various experiences suggest that empirical data alone do not constitute the most important factor in decisions to adopt new programs (Sechrest, 1993).

The effective introduction of new programs requires both the support of and pressure from school administrators. Pressure is necessary to change the status quo of organizational functioning and to push for high-quality implementation; otherwise, the more difficult aspects of many programs are eliminated, and interventions become watered down. Administrative support is also essential: There must be sufficient resources available to conduct the program, in the form of materials, consultation, and training; and some form of compensation and recognition for teachers must be provided. Both the initial implementation of a program and its maintenance after a trial period are highly dependent on the level of professional development and assistance provided to change agents.

Finally, the more complex the intervention, the longer it will take change agents to incorporate new procedures fully into their repertoires. Sufficient time must be allotted for staff training and continual consultation, and it may take several years before all the critical features of a program are successfully mastered. One-shot workshops and brief in-service training are insufficient to support the introduction of complex interventions.

Problems inevitably arise when new procedures are tried. Advance planning to anticipate difficulties and, in particular, to permit change agents to solve problems collaboratively and to develop their own solutions increases the likelihood of program maintenance and allows school staff greater ownership of the new program. Ownership is also enhanced when teachers are allowed to modify programs to fit their schedules, organizational routines, and student bodies. In fact, program flexibility in this regard seems essential. Interventions that ignore the realities of school life are doomed to failure.

Community support for change increases the overall chances that problems of implementation will be resolved and programs will endure. The generation of active parental support helps facilitate change. Program maintenance is also fostered when change agents perceive obvious bene-fits from the intervention. In this vein, research data that illustrate the practical significance of obtained changes are most helpful.

One of the most effective dissemination efforts to date in school-based prevention involves the PMHP project, first mentioned in Chapter 2 (Cowen, 1980). Beginning in the mid-1970s, PMHP, a secondary preven-tion program emphasizing early screening and identification of school maladjustment, has sought to influence other schools to implement similar projects in their communities by conducting extensive workshops, devel-oping regional dissemination centers, encouraging state-level support for new programs, and providing consultation and resources to interested parties. This dissemination effort has been highly successful. PMHP has influenced the development of programs in more than 300 schools that annually provide services to more than 10,000 schoolchildren (Cowen, Hightower, Johnson, Sarno, & Weissberg, 1989). Examples of other successful dissemination efforts may be found in the work of Pentz (1986) and Rohrbach, Graham, and Hansen (1993).

IMPORTANCE OF
PROGRAM IMPLEMENTATION

Implementation refers to what a program actually consists of in prac-tice. Implementation is not an all-or-none process; rather, it exists in degrees and reflects the extent to which a change agent delivers an intervention in the prescribed fashion, abstaining from adding extra, nonprescribed, elements. Program implementation is sometimes called treatment adherence, program integrity, or program fidelity.

Systematic study of the implementation process requires the specification and operational definition of crucial components of a program and the development of objective procedures to assess implementation quality. Research on these issues is just beginning for clinical (McGrew, Bond, Dieten, & Salyers, 1994) as well as preventive interventions. Some researchers in the latter area have relied on self-reports from change agents, which have their customary limitations, whereas others have made observations of actual program processes. Regardless of the research technique, however, data are accumulating regarding the importance of studying implementation for two reasons: (a) Implementation can vary dramatically across settings, and (b) the quality of implementation is related to program outcomes.

Studies indicate that the level of program implementation is never 100% and is often seriously deficient. One study found that 67% of teachers did not implement a crucial element of a substance abuse program related to parent involvement (Flannery & Torquati, 1993); in another, only 46% of teachers were considered to have implemented a program effectively (Taggart, Bush, Zuckerman, & Theiss, 1990); in a third, teachers omitted 23% to 50% of the proscribed program activities (Smith, McCormick, Steckler, & McLeroy, 1993); in a fourth, only 22% of teachers were judged to be high implementers, whereas 41% and 37% were moderate and low implementers, respectively (Resnicow et al., 1992). In a fifth study, only 21% of trained teachers actually implemented all elements of a new program (Rohrbach et al., 1993), and in a sixth study, only one third of the teachers who had initially indicated they would implement a tobacco prevention program were offering any part of the intervention in their classes 2 years later (Gingiss, Gottlieb, & Brink, 1994). Finally, Tobler (1986) found that among 22 drug-abuse prevention studies assessing the degree of implementation, those reporting proper implementation achieved a mean effect size 0.34 greater than those reporting poor implementation. This was a substantial difference, because the mean effect achieved by all 143 programs in Tobler's review was 0.30.

Moreover, when investigators study the relationship between program implementation and outcome, data indicate either (a) that significant results occur for prevention programs only when the intervention is properly implemented (Ross, Luepker, Nelson, Saavedra, & Hubbard,

1991; Taggart et al., 1990) or (b) that much stronger results are obtained under circumstances of more complete implementation (Botvin, Baker, Dusenbury, Botvin, & Diaz, 1995; Connell, Turner, & Mason, 1985; Rohrbach et al., 1993). These studies confirm the commonsense notion that anything worth doing is worth doing well.

The term *Type III error,* which has been coined in relation to program implementation, refers to the evaluation of a program that has not been effectively implemented (Scanlon, Horst, Nay, Schmidt, & Waller, 1977). In other words, we cannot make a fair assessment of a program unless we know the extent to which its essential elements have been administered. Essential elements are those components that are believed to be responsible for change.

Although several factors can affect the quality of program implementation, effective training and support of change agents is fundamental. Huberman and Miles (1984) found that "large-scale, change-bearing innovations lived or died by the amount and quality of assistance that their users received once the change process was underway" (p. 273). The training programs that appear most successful follow principles similar to those for effective teaching: Provide trainees with clear demonstrations of the behaviors to be learned, monitor their progress as they practice new skills, and deliver consistent support and reinforcement for efforts to change.

THE FANTASY OF
UNTREATED CONTROL GROUPS

Another related issue involves the need to monitor interventions received by those in control conditions. Because so many preventive programs currently exist in the schools, most studies of newly introduced programs are more likely to compare those who receive the new intervention with those receiving the standard or routine program, rather than with those receiving no program. As a result, there are probably few situations in which completely untreated control conditions exist. For example, one evaluation of a drug-abuse prevention program discovered that there was an alternative program being offered in *100% of the control classrooms* (Ary et al., 1990). Other investigators undoubtedly would also uncover alternative interventions in the schools if they were to look for them.

When alternative treatments are being compared, the effect sizes obtained from outcome evaluations will probably be substantially lower than those obtained in treatment versus true no-treatment comparisons (Kazdin, Bass, Ayers, & Rodgers, 1990). Therefore, there is a need to ascertain the existence and implementation of any alternative treatments. Although the implementation of treatment and control conditions is discussed here under the topic of program diffusion, these issues are relevant at all stages of prevention research, beginning when pilot programs are first being evaluated.

In summary, in many outcome evaluations controls receive more treatment than expected owing to the existence of standard programming, and experimental children receive less because of problems involved in implementation. These circumstances work against the finding of strong effects for preventive interventions because the assumptions behind treatment-versus-control comparisons are not usually met. This is important to keep in mind in the development of a fair standard for evaluation of new programs.

This chapter has only scratched the surface of a complex and important topic. For additional information about different aspects of program diffusion, interested readers may want to refer other sources, including Fullan (1991, 1992), House (1974), Rogers (1983), Scheirer (1990), Stolz (1981), and Weissberg et al. (1989).

SUMMARY

In brief, program diffusion involves the extent to which effective programs are identified and used in schools. It includes four phases: dissemination, adoption, implementation, and maintenance. Unfortunately, the relevant factors at each stage of program diffusion have not been systematically evaluated. Implementation, or what a program actually consists of in practice, is an important but generally overlooked aspect of program evaluation. Data clearly indicate that incompletely or incorrectly implemented programs achieve fewer benefits. If social scientists want schools to use empirically validated interventions, they need to give greater attention to program diffusion.

7

CURRENT STATUS
AND FUTURE DIRECTIONS

In the preceding chapters I have described the goals, methods, and outcomes of school-based prevention in several different areas. In this chapter, I attempt to synthesize this information in order to reach some general conclusions and to discuss future directions. My general conclusions are presented first, followed by discussion of some methodological guidelines for future research. In the last section of the chapter, I offer a few suggestions and predictions about future work.

GENERAL CONCLUSIONS

School-based prevention is a very young science: 74% of all published research studies on the behavioral impacts of school-based prevention have appeared since 1980. Given its short history, it is not surprising that more work needs to be done and only tentative conclusions can be reached. Nevertheless, school-based research has come a long way in a very short time. Several areas have demonstrated rapid growth in both methodological and conceptual sophistication and program impacts.

The following conclusions and recommendations are based on the results of the better-controlled investigations discussed in earlier chapters. Although these studies are in the minority, they are models for future work and indicate what can be achieved. The summaries at the ends of the chapters indicate the specific conclusions that can be reached in given areas. My intent here is to provide on overview of the current status of school-based prevention. I revisit only a few previous studies to illustrate some of the data supporting each conclusion.

Major Trends

There have been two major trends in the focus of prevention research, and these trends suggest which strategies have been the most effective. The first involves a shift in which individual factors are important; the second involves targeting factors beyond the individual.

Skills training. Initially, prevention programs were begun in different areas with the hope that improving knowledge would change behavior. Such programs were not effective in the areas where they were tried, including AIDS and sex education, drug-use prevention, pregnancy prevention, and health education. Researchers then shifted their attention away from informational programs to emphasize skills training. Some of the most commonly targeted skills include assertiveness, communication, self-control and self-management, decision making, and goal setting. Skills training must be systematic to be effective, and most programs use a social learning training approach that includes a reoccurring loop of instruction, modeling, behavioral rehearsal, and feedback until mastery is achieved. Many programs including skills-training components have been effective, leading Allensworth (1993) to state, "Acquisition of basic skills at appropriate ages appears to be a primary component of all prevention" (p. 17).

Targeting environmental factors. The second shift that has occurred involves extending the focus of intervention from individual to environmental factors. Peers, parents, aspects of the school and classroom environment, the media, and social norms have been targeted most frequently. These environmental factors have been chosen because researchers have identified risk factors in these domains. For example, risk factors in the individual, peer group, school, family, and community are all associated with drug use. Because risk factors can have multiplicative effects, programs that effectively reduce more risk factors should be more effective. In other words, there may be limits on the success that can be achieved if only individual factors are targeted for intervention.

Environmental interventions are a two-edged sword. On the one hand, they are difficult to implement; it is usually easier to gain access to groups of children for an individual-level intervention than it is to change the classroom or school environment or to involve parents. We currently lack a good taxonomy of environments, making it difficult to identify what and how things should be changed and how such changes should be assessed

(Kelly, 1988). On the other hand, environmental change may be critical for reaching more of the target population and for maintaining program impact. For instance, once a school food service introduces healthier foods into its menu these changes affect the entire population of those who use the cafeteria each year. Similarly, if parents change, they can become a continual source of support and reinforcement for their children's new behaviors.

Schools are a natural home base for prevention programming. Millions of schoolchildren are exposed to programs with a preventive focus each year in the United States. Various factors coalesce to induce educators to offer sex and AIDS education, drug-use prevention programs, physical health education, and various interventions directed at personal and social growth. Unfortunately, the overwhelming majority of programs currently used in the schools have not been subjected to careful evaluation. As a result, their behavioral impacts are questionable.

At the same time, research indicates that some prevention programs are successful. Therefore, the challenge is to clarify how effective programs should be packaged and how schools can be convinced to accept these offerings to ensure that high-quality programs are institutionalized into the schools.

Prevention has positive benefits. School-based prevention takes many forms. Primary prevention consists of person- or environment-centered programs involving all children, only those at risk, or only those undergoing important life transitions. Secondary prevention involves prompt intervention with children who have subclinical problems. Researchers have been able to translate these different approaches into viable programs that have significant positive effects. Prevention can work in four different ways: (a) by preventing the initial occurrence of problems, (b) by delaying the onset of difficulties, (c) by reducing the severity of difficulties that do appear, and (d) by preventing early problems from becoming worse. There are several examples throughout this book of how programs have achieved one or more of these outcomes.

Prevention achieves outcomes equal to established interventions in the behavioral, social, and educational sciences. This might be the most surprising of all findings. Lipsey and Wilson (1993) report that the mean effect size attained across 9,400 interventions in the social and behavioral sciences and in education was 0.47, with a standard deviation of 0.29. Many preventive programs whose impacts can be translated into effect sizes have achieved results of similar or greater magnitude. This is an impressive achievement, because children involved in primary prevention who are functioning within the normal range to begin with or those participating in secondary prevention who have minor difficulties do not have much opportunity to change dramatically. In other words, prevention clearly has merit as a strategy for achieving change in target populations.

Prevention achieves results of practical significance. Preventive interventions can produce meaningful changes in schoolchildren's lives. This is most clearly evident in successful academic programs (Chapter 4), drug-use prevention programs (Chapter 3), and some interventions to prevent behavioral and social problems (Chapter 2). Some of the more dramatic findings include the following. High-risk children who receive early childhood educational services before first grade and whose families benefit from a variety of support services are subsequently less likely to fail a school grade, to be placed in special education classes, or to drop out of school. Some of these findings are apparent through 12 years of follow-up, and some programs have simultaneously reduced behavioral school problems and enhanced academic functioning. Programs designed to train students to resist peer and media pressures to use drugs and more comprehensive programs targeting peers, families, and the media have been successful in substantially reducing the number of children who use drugs and the quantity of drugs they use. Finally, programs to prevent behavioral problems have been effective in reducing aggression and other forms of acting-out behavior. These findings are important because acting-out behaviors constitute one of the most serious and intractable forms of childhood and adolescent dysfunction.

Health promotion programs have potential. Although some may disagree (e.g., Institute of Medicine, 1994), health promotion deserves continued attention as a preventive strategy. Health promotion has value in and of itself in terms of enhancing personal and social functioning, or psychological well-being, but for such programs to be viewed as preventive interventions, the link between promotion and reduction of problems needs to be demonstrated. Several successful person- and environment-centered programs that emphasize health promotion have been cited throughout this book. These include interventions to enhance family functioning and to help teachers improve the classroom environment (Chapter 4), programs to teach students assertiveness and peer resistance skills as part of drug use prevention (Chapter 3), and some interventions directed at physical health education (Chapter 5) and behavioral and social problems (Chapter 2).

Health promotion programs seem to be most effective when they focus on objectives that are incompatible with maladaptive behaviors, or, phrased another way, when they promote behaviors that specifically reduce risk. For instance, effective resistance skills are incompatible with accepting a cigarette from a friend; a child who chooses healthy foods for lunch is not eating unhealthy foods. An additional benefit of health promotion lies in the possibility that health promotion programs may identify more protective factors that can be used to inform future prevention research. Restricting research on protective factors to a pathological framework will limit the nature and number of protective factors that will be found.

Quality of implementation matters. There is accumulating evidence that validates the commonsense notion that something worth doing is worth doing well. The quality of implementation, or how well a program is actually put into practice, significantly affects outcomes. Data clearly indicate that programs produce fewer benefits if they are not implemented completely or correctly. In fact, prevention programs that have been transported to new settings for wider-scale application have never achieved 100% implementation. Therefore, it is entirely possible that some prevention programs have been discarded as ineffective when in reality they have failed because they have been compromised; the true, intended programs were never conducted appropriately. We can no longer ignore the implementation process of prevention programs. Studying the relationship between implementation and outcome should become a routine matter in future studies.

Characteristics of Effective Programs

Although it is important to know that, in general, prevention works, we need more information on the specificity of program effects. Important questions involve the what, who, why, where, when, and how of prevention (Gullotta, 1994), all of which need further clarification. Because the mechanisms of change have not been determined, only a few tentative conclusions can be reached regarding the relationship between program characteristics and outcomes. Two of these conclusions follow.

Programs that have effects that are durable over time tend to be intensive, multicomponent, multilevel interventions. Many different types of interventions have produced immediate positive effects, but those with more enduring effects have been multidimensional programs that have targeted multiple individual, social, and organizational factors. In contrast, brief interventions tend to yield benefits that are more likely to dissipate over time. This makes perfect sense. There are no magic prevention pills; if there were a brief, one-shot approach that could produce lasting and substantial changes in people's lives, someone would have discovered it by now. Behavioral and social changes are complex phenomena, and multidimensional, multilevel interventions acknowledge this complexity.

In some cases, such as drug education, it is not program intensity but persistence that matters most. That is, interventions that are present over multiple school years, that include booster sessions, or that are offered in conjunction with ongoing communitywide prevention activities are more likely to produce results that last. A critical feature in this respect might be that different factors affect children's behaviors at different times. Therefore, an intervention spread out over time is more likely to fit children's maturational and developmental needs.

Although the timing of interventions seems important, the critical periods when programs are more or less effective are unknown. The presence of early problems often predicts later problems for several behaviors, such as aggression, learning difficulties, drug taking, unprotected sexual intercourse, and poor peer relations, but our knowledge about the initial manifestations of these problems differs. For instance, intervention to prevent learning problems in low-income children should begin before first grade, and earlier and more sustained interventions have been more effective than others (see Chapter 4). To forestall the onset of sexual intercourse, intervention must begin before youth begin such activity, but the age at which this occurs varies depending on the demographics of the target population (Alan Guttmacher Institute, 1994). Researchers are just beginning to assemble epidemiological data regarding the prevalence of drug use at different ages (Hansen, 1992), and, once again, variations occur across populations. For many behavioral and social problems, the specific onset of difficulties is not clear-cut.

BASIC RESEARCH ISSUES

Volumes have been written about prevention research; the following discussion selectively highlights some important topics. In this section I present a general perspective on prevention research, followed by a discussion of some specific methodological issues.

General Stages in Prevention Research

There are several ways to characterize the stages involved in prevention research (Cowen, 1986; Flay, 1986; Institute of Medicine, 1994). The six stages described below illustrate the different types and levels of research that are relevant:

1. *Develop usable theories and hypotheses.* This stage draws upon the multidisciplinary character of prevention and involves the critical examination of what is currently known about the development and malleability of problems and competencies in different groups. Basic and applied research findings and theories from many disciplines are relevant. As noted in Chapter 1, much recent prevention research centers on modifying risk or protective factors in an effort to promote healthy functioning and prevent future problems. The basic task, then, in this stage, is to develop a theoretical or conceptual framework to guide the intervention.

2. *Conduct pilot programs.* The aim here is to demonstrate positive impact through internally valid program evaluations. There are many features relevant to internal validity that vary in importance depending on the particular research study. Essentially, the intent is to make a strong connection between an intervention and its effects by ruling out plausible rival explanations for the obtained data.

3. *Replicate and confirm the success of pilot studies.* Success at this stage increases the confidence that initial results can be accepted. Given the limitations of most applied research, it is important to replicate prior findings.

4. *Identify active program components.* At this stage the researcher assesses how different features of the intervention contribute to different outcomes. Some elements may not be powerful enough to achieve their intended effects and will have to be enhanced, whereas other components may be unnecessary and can be eliminated. The latter is important because briefer interventions are more likely to be accepted in more settings.

5. *Conduct large-scale field trials.* This stage often entails conceptual and procedural refinements in program design to demonstrate external validity. Does the program work for different groups in different settings and when the program is conducted by different personnel?

6. *Promote program diffusion.* In this last stage, the researcher attempts to convince others to adopt and use the intervention in their settings. The most effective programs are promoted so that as many schools as possible use them. The hope is that diffusion will be successful on a communitywide basis.

Ideally, the above stages are sequential, but in reality they seldom are, because many administrative, financial, and political factors affect what research can be done, how and when, and under what circumstances the findings are applied or extended. This is not necessarily disastrous. Sometimes, a large-scale field trial (Stage 5) provides new information not discernible in previous, less ambitious, studies. Results of replications (Stage 3) might suggest the need to refine program theory, and new theoretical formulations can occur at any time to stimulate a new round of research. Finally, even if research on all previous stages has not been completed, program diffusion needs to be studied at least on a preliminary basis because so few empirical data currently exist on this topic. Nevertheless, the above scenario describes a natural progression of research, and one can assess the general maturity of a field by observing at what level of research most work is being conducted or is needed.

School-based prevention is at different stages of research depending on the area. For example, some research regarding drug-use prevention and academic programs and a few health education programs has proceeded to Stage 5. A series of programmatic research studies has led groups to examine the applicability of some programs on a wide scale. For example, some studies involve multiple schools or school systems and several hundred to several thousand participants (see Chapter 3). As a result, a few interventions have been studied systematically across a variety of school settings and populations to support the program's external validity. Researchers in both drug and health education have been in the forefront in Stage 6 activities—studying program diffusion, particularly the implementation process. Much other school-based research remains at Stages 1, 2, and 3 as theories and programs are developed, pilot tested, and then reexamined in replication trials. Such work is essential to provide a firm grounding for later studies.

There is a major need for research in Stage 3 for all types of programs. The effective elements of prevention programs have not been identified. There are multiple components to most programs, and researchers are only now beginning to compare programs containing different elements to determine their relative contributions to outcomes. One implication is that current theories supporting prevention will likely be revised. The active ingredients of interventions are suggested (or should be) by program theory. Multicomponent programs are developed based on the belief that each feature is necessary for the attainment of program goals. In all probability, the results of future studies will challenge these assumptions for some interventions. Some program elements will not demonstrate intended effects, and some positive outcomes will occur for unforeseen reasons. The behavioral and social sciences contain several examples of surprise findings that occurred when programs were inspected to see why they were effective. There is no reason to believe that the field of prevention will be any exception.

We do know, however, what does not work: Information, by itself, is not an effective preventive strategy. Gains in knowledge have not led to significant and consistent behavior change in any preventive area. Youth do need accurate information to guide their subsequent behaviors, but the imparting of knowledge is not the crucial ingredient leading to behavioral change.

Guidelines for Prevention Research

Although prevention programs vary widely in their target populations and objectives, there is general agreement about what features should be present in evaluations for maximum benefit. Several authors have offered suggestions to improve future research (Coie et al., 1993; Flay, 1986; Heller, Price, & Sher, 1980; Institute of Medicine, 1994; Jason, Thompson, & Rose, 1986; Lorion, 1990; Price, Cowen, Lorion, & Ramos-McKay, 1989; Rolf, 1985). A synthesis of their comments and the addition of some new material produces a set of 12 guidelines for the design and evaluation of preventive interventions. These are listed in Table 7.1. These recommendations do not, of course, cover all methodological issues; they are offered here in light of the characteristics of current research.

There are multiple operations related to each guideline, which, in turn, relate to different stages of prevention research. For example, the first six guidelines in Table 7.1 are relevant in demonstrating the internal validity of research. These guidelines are most germane to the first four stages of prevention research (development of theory, pilot programming, replication trials, identification of active program components). Guideline 10 is relevant to Stage 5 in terms of the demonstration of external validity, and Guideline 12 involves the sixth and last phase, assuring that effective programs are used by others. No single study, of course, can accomplish

TABLE 7.1 Basic Guidelines for Conducting Preventive Interventions

---

 1. Develop or use theory to drive the research.
 2. Clarify specific goals and objectives.
 3. Operationalize intervention procedures.
 4. Select an appropriate target population.
 5. Evaluate program implementation.
 6. Measure relevant outcomes adequately.
 7. Assess practical significance of outcomes.
 8. Follow up on treatment effects.
 9. Evaluate costs, benefits, and cost-effectiveness.
10. Assess the generality of findings.
11. Examine how different participants respond to intervention.
12. Plan for program diffusion.

---

all the tasks outlined in Table 7.1, but different studies can be devoted to different objectives. The following discussion focuses on a few guidelines; additional information is available in the sources named above.

The value of theory in guiding research cannot be overestimated. A good theory specifies a model for intervention and analysis. Theory helps in the identification of an appropriate target population, the design of the actual program, the specification of outcomes, and the determination of which variables should be analyzed and how. As a result, theory-driven research is preferred, because it permits the researcher to explain the results in a coherent and logical fashion.

Guidelines 2 (Clarify specific goals), 6 (Measure outcomes adequately), and 7 (Assess practical significance) are particularly important for the assessment of a program's preventive impact. Some research has been conducted without clear and specific goals or objectives, so that even when positive results are obtained it is not clear what, if anything, has been prevented. Outcome measures must be valid, reliable, and sensitive enough to detect relatively small changes in behavior. Children involved in primary prevention are functioning within the normal range. One cannot assume that instruments used in clinical studies with dysfunctional populations are sufficiently sensitive to measure change that occur at subclinical levels.

Practical significance refers to whether or not a meaningful change in adjustment or behavior has occurred. It is possible to achieve statistical significance on outcomes based on only small or trivial changes in functioning. Whenever possible, investigators should demonstrate the practical significance of obtained outcomes.

By definition, prevention has a future time perspective. Intervention occurs in the present to forestall future problems. Therefore, it is incumbent on investigators to document the durability of program effects. Actually, many follow-up studies suggest that the effects from preventive programs do not dissipate over time. Relatively short follow-ups are the rule, however, and the majority of studies have not collected any follow-up data.

Major considerations for external validity involve the setting (urban, suburban, rural), educational level (elementary, junior high, high school—if the intervention is appropriate at each of these levels), and cultural diversity among students. Moreover, are there indications that the program has been offered on a large scale such that it is appropriate for many schools? Programs conducted in only a few schools may not be generalizable.

Finally, the characteristics of the change agent are also important. Can others be trained to conduct the program appropriately (e.g., teachers, perhaps in combination with peers or parents)? If an intervention has been evaluated only when it has been offered by the original program developers and their carefully trained staff, the application to real-world settings is questionable.

Interventions should be evaluated based on the assumption that the same approach will not work for everybody (Guideline 11). Preventionists are now beginning to document how different members of target populations respond to interventions. Such information is critical to the improvement of the next generation of programs. The following variables have been most frequently related to program impacts in different studies: age, gender, relevant skills, and risk status. This is not a long list of variables, but most research designs have not examined the influence of participant characteristics on outcomes. Therefore, it is important to plan program evaluations to assess how interventions affect different program participants.

Students' racial or ethnic status has *not* been a factor in outcomes among most studies investigating this matter. This is encouraging. Some prevention programs have been effective regardless of children's ethnic or cultural groups, and, when necessary, investigators have been able to customize interventions so that they are culturally sensitive (e.g., Jemmott, Jemmott, & Fong, 1992).

If prevention is to have a prominent place in schools, then investigators must devote more attention to all four phases of program diffusion:

dissemination, adoption, implementation, and institutionalization or maintenance (Guideline 12). Unfortunately, a large gap exists between researchers who evaluate programs and school personnel who might consider using these interventions.

Program diffusion, the last stage in prevention research, assumes the existence of programs of proven effectiveness that should be tried on a communitywide scale. However, there are few, if any, school-based programs that meet this standard. Slavin, Karweit, and Wasik (1994) have recommended several academic programs, and there may be a few drug programs, that should receive more large-scale testing. For the most part, however, it is premature at this time to advocate that current prevention programs be diffused into schools.

It is essential that only the very best programs be tried on a wide scale. Children should not be exposed to interventions whose positive and negative effects are not clearly understood. Moreover, there is the danger of overselling preventive programs. Schinke (1994) has noted that as prevention programs become more visible, they will also be scrutinized more carefully. Therefore, ethics demand that we learn more about the factors affecting outcomes for preventive programs before we attempt to market these interventions throughout the country.

It is now more prudent to examine basic issues related to program diffusion. There are several questions that have to be answered empirically. For instance, what factors influence schools to adopt programs and what factors affect program implementation and maintenance? Schools usually make adoption decisions about curricula in categorical fashion (i.e., Should we use this health education curricula?). Would schools accept combined programs that have multiple aims (i.e., programs designed to prevent both drug use and behavioral problems)?

Although it is axiomatic that prevention is a more cost-effective approach for a wide variety of problems than the treatment of established dysfunction, there have been only a few empirical demonstrations that the benefits obtained from intervention outweigh its costs (e.g., Barnett, 1990; Connell, Turner, & Mason, 1985; Perry et al., 1988; Slavin et al., 1994). More work on this topic is needed. Assessing the costs and benefits of preventive programs is challenging because of the difficulties in quantifying behavioral and social outcomes, but such assessment could be very important for the widespread diffusion of interventions. Schools often weigh the costs and benefits of adopting new programs (see Chapter 6), but often do so informally. Explicit cost-benefit and cost-effectiveness analyses could help schools decide whether or not new programs are worth while. State and federal educational agencies could also find comparisons of costs and benefits helpful regarding funding or sanctioning of different programs.

Finally, more process research is needed. Process studies will help investigators identify core features of their interventions and examine to what extent these features have been implemented as planned. The resultant data should lead to more careful operationalization of interventions and the development of program manuals that, in turn, will aid others who wish to replicate programs.

In summary, we need to know exactly what was done, and how well, in different programs; how different members of the target population responded in the short and long term; and what mechanisms might account for the obtained results. No single study can provide answers to all these questions, but research that carefully addresses any of them will make the next generation of prevention studies much more interpretable.

FINAL OBSERVATIONS

I conclude this chapter with some miscellaneous observations about the current and future status of school-based prevention research.

Need for Prevention Training

In large part, the science of prevention has been introduced into schools by a small cadre of researchers who have the necessary expertise. Most teachers, administrators, school psychologists, and social workers first learn about prevention during their interactions with these researchers. School staff could make greater contributions to the development of new interventions, however, if they received appropriate preparation during their professional training. Therefore, to ensure wider support for school-based efforts, training in prevention should become a regular part of the training sequence in professional programs, most particularly in education, the behavioral and social sciences, and health education.

Schools' Inability to Do It All

A large proportion of all prevention for children and adolescents has been based in schools, and more work is needed on community-based programming. It is true that schools are an important influence on development; the average child who graduates from high school has spent approximately one third of her or his waking life in school. During this same period, however, 66% of the child's waking time has been spent outside of school. Therefore, it is reasonable to expect some limits on the impact of school-based interventions, particularly when there are also out-of-school influences on target behaviors or problems. For example, youth receive so many cultural and social messages supporting the use of alcohol that is difficult to combat these influences through a single drug intervention. Clearly, schools cannot bear all the responsibility for prevention. More community-based preventive initiatives are needed to modify more of the influences upon children's growth and development.

Contributions From Basic Research

As noted in Chapter 1, our knowledge about relevant risk factors and protective factors, including their possible interactions and mechanisms of action, is sketchy. We need better ways to identify groups at risk for different problems at different ages and to quantify risk levels whenever possible for different children. We also must identify more protective factors.

Future prevention research will also be greatly served by research on developmental pathways. Basically, pathways are life histories that clarify the important stages of development and indicate when and how critical shifts toward positive or negative developmental trajectories are possible. For example, all other things being equal, children who acquire basic academic skills in the early grades are on a positive academic course, whereas those with early learning difficulties are on a negative developmental course and at risk for more serious problems. Intervention with the latter group could reverse this negative trajectory. The efficiency of interventions is in large part determined by how much is known about what to do, when, with whom, and in the context of the child's prior development and current family and school.

Pathways are likely to differ across individual behaviors, collections of behaviors that constitute disorders, competencies, and populations. Data that begin to clarify the developmental pathways of adjustment and maladjustment for different groups of children over time and to specify which risk factors and protective factors influence development will be extremely helpful to preventionists who seek to design more efficient and effective interventions.

Coordination of Preventive Programs

Most school-based prevention is categorical in nature, that is, it focuses on one type of program and goal (academic, drug-use prevention, health, etc.). Evidence is beginning to appear, however, that outcomes for some interventions generalize across domains. Programs to prevent behavioral problems have had positive effects on academic functioning, and some academic programs also have been shown to prevent behavioral problems (see Chapters 2 and 4). Categorical programming could be replaced by efforts to integrate and coordinate different offerings more efficiently. For example, behavioral programs could be offered following academic programs designed to ensure that children acquire basic academic proficiency. Positive behavioral benefits accruing from the academic intervention might either reduce the need for a subsequent behavioral intervention or augment its effects. At the same time, academic intervention could continue for those who need it as the behavioral intervention is started. An interlocking system of interventions would assure that more children receive attention in relation to their needs, and it is logical to consider academic, health, and behavioral programs as overlapping rather than as isolated interventions.

One of the current National Health Promotion and Disease Prevention Objectives (U.S. Department of Health and Human Services, 1989) is to increase to 75% the proportion of primary and secondary schools that provide comprehensive, sequential, developmentally appropriate health education from kindergarten through Grade 12. Different prevention programs would be welcome under the umbrella of school health education providing that the multiple disciplines currently involved in prevention could agree on a collaborative enterprise. At present, such comprehensive programming is an ideal goal, but it will be instructive to see how schools can coordinate and integrate different preventive curricula.

The Context for Preventive School-Based Services

How can prevention play a more prominent role in schools? Although much prevention occurs in schools, it often occupies a peripheral position. Prevention programs need to be more thoroughly integrated into school programs and curricula. The ideal arrangement is perhaps some form of a pyramid of services (Weissberg, Caplan, & Harwood, 1991). Primary prevention would be the first line of defense for all problems, secondary prevention the second line, and psychotherapy the third. To the extent that research supports such a position, all young schoolchildren would participate in primary prevention programs designed to promote growth and prevent problems. Primary prevention will not help all children, and those with subclinical problems could benefit from secondary prevention targeted specifically for them. In turn, secondary prevention may not be effective for those with the most serious difficulties, and traditional counseling and psychotherapy services could be offered. Unless substantial changes are made in the provision of school-based services, large numbers of children who will otherwise develop problems of varying degrees of severity will not receive any systematic attention.

The Neglect of Teachers

Although there are many preventive programs for schoolchildren, teachers have been ignored as a target group. There is a strong need for preventive programs specifically designed for teachers. Currently, only one half to two thirds of teachers teach for more than 7 years (Fullan, 1992), and almost all teachers seriously consider leaving their profession at one point or another (Durlak, 1983). There have been a few interventions to reduce stress and burnout among teachers after the fact, but programs are needed to prevent such outcomes from developing in the first place.

Teachers need more assistance during their professional training and on the job. Few would disagree with the assertion that teacher education programs do not adequately prepare teachers for their chosen career. Too many new teachers experience a baptism by fire as they deal with the multiple rigors and demands of teaching, and many become stressed, overwhelmed, and disillusioned. Furthermore, the typical classroom teacher is assigned too many students who are too varied in ability, and who demonstrate multiple and diverse personal, social, and even physical needs. Teachers' assumption of added responsibilities for assisting pupils is not met with concomitant preparation during teacher training programs or adequate administrative and social support in most school systems. In fact, many of the prevention programs discussed in this text increase teachers' responsibilities for student growth and development, thus potentially increasing the burden of teaching.

There is no easy solution to the teachers' plight. Schools of education must be revamped so that their graduates possess more effective skills for managing and teaching children, and so that they enter the profession with an ideology that fosters change and experimentation. School districts must take more seriously the notion of professional staff development and offer more meaningful opportunities to teachers for collaboration and input into school policies and procedures. Major educational reform may be necessary to achieve these ends, and several authors offer sound ideas in this regard (Fullan, 1992; Goodlad, 1991; Sarason, 1990, 1993). Ultimately, the extent to which prevention programs truly take hold in schools will be largely determined by how well the needs of teachers are addressed. As Sarason (1993) has noted, "If conditions for productive growth do not exist for teachers, they cannot create and sustain those conditions for students" (pp. 256-257).

SUMMARY

School-based prevention works. It works in the sense that prevention programs produce results equal in magnitude to other change strategies in mental health and education. It works in the sense that several interventions have produced meaningful changes in schoolchildren's lives that are durable over time. The research literature is far from definitive, however, and more work must be done to strengthen confidence in program outcomes. Success has been uneven across programs, and we do not know the specific factors that account for differential program impacts. As Sechrest (1993) notes: "Prevention is not something that can be settled once and for all. It will require continuous research efforts" (p. 668). It is my hope that this book will stimulate further interest and activity in school-based prevention.

APPENDIX:
A PRIMER ON EFFECT SIZES

In several cases throughout this book, particularly in Chapters 2 and 4, study outcomes are presented in the form of a standardized mean effect size, or simply an effect size (ES). This appendix provides some basic information to help the reader understand what these data involve and how they can be interpreted.

WHAT IS AN EFFECT SIZE?

A standardized ES is a statistic reflecting how much more change occurred in an experimental than in a comparison or control group following an intervention. ESs are calculated in such a way that positive scores indicate the experimental group was superior to the control group and negative scores have a reverse meaning. That is, an ES equals the posttreatment mean of the control group subtracted from the corresponding mean of the experimental group and then divided by either the standard deviation of the control group or the pooled standard deviation of both groups. An ES is calculated for each outcome measure in a study, and then these ESs are usually averaged across all outcomes to yield an average effect per study. ESs can then be averaged across studies when investigations in a similar area are reviewed. Because ESs are standardized (i.e., calculated in terms of standard deviation units) they are comparable across studies. All other things being equal, an intervention that yields an ES of 0.40 is twice as powerful as one that produces an ES of 0.20.

An ES can be of any value, but most fall between −1.0 and +1.0. There is no absolute criterion in evaluating the magnitude of effects. The grand mean effect drawn from 156 reviews of 9,400 interventions in the social and behavioral sciences and in education is 0.47 (SD = .28), which affords some comparison (Lipsey & Wilson, 1993). This grand mean was drawn from many different types of programs, and in many cases interventions were offered to dysfunctional populations. ESs should be higher in the latter cases, because these groups have more room or opportunity to change. Such is not the case, however, in preventive programs when populations do not initially have any serious adjustment problems. At any rate, ESs that fall within one standard deviation of the grand mean of 0.47 (e.g., ESs between 0.19 and 0.75) reported by Lipsey and Wilson (1993) are within the range typically achieved by interventions.

PRACTICAL SIGNIFICANCE
OF EFFECT SIZES

There is no straightforward relationship between the magnitude of an ES and its practical significance. Rosenthal and Rubin (1982) have described a way of translating ESs to assess their practical significance. A standardized ES is simply divided by 2 and the resulting figure represents the relative percentage difference in success rates between the experimental and control groups. For example, an ES of 0.40 indicates that the experimental group experienced a 20% higher success rate than the control group (60% vs. 40%). If the intervention had no effect, then the success rates for both groups would equal 50%. (The success rates for both groups always add to 100%.)

In other words, an ES does not have to be large to have practical significance. Much depends on the type of outcome measure on which the effect is calculated. For example, if the ES is only .20, then the success rate for the experimental and control groups would be 55% versus 45%, respectively (0.20 divided by 2 and interpreted as a percentage). This 10% difference could be very important if it is based on outcomes assessing school dropout rates, rates of serious behavioral problems, or the like. Several sources discuss ESs and their use in meta-analyses that evaluate the impact of interventions in quantitative terms (Durlak, 1994; Durlak & Lipsey, 1991; Light & Pillemer, 1984).

REFERENCES

Alan Guttmacher Institute. (1994). *Sex and America's teenagers.* New York: Author.

Allensworth, D. D. (1993). Health education: State of the art. *Journal of School Health, 63,* 14-20.

Alpert-Gillis, L. J., Pedro-Carroll, J. L., & Cowen, E. L. (1989). The Child of Divorce Intervention Program: Development, implementation, and evaluation of a program for young urban children. *Journal of Consulting and Clinical Psychology, 57,* 583-589.

Archambault, F. X., Jr. (1989). Instructional setting and other design features of compensatory education programs. In R. E. Slavin, N. L. Karweit, & N. A. Madden (Eds.), *Effective programs for students at risk* (pp. 220-263). Needham Heights, MA: Allyn & Bacon.

Ary, D. V., Biglan, A., Glasgow, R., Zoref, L., Black, C., Ochs, L., Severson, H., Kelly, R., Weissman, W., Lichtenstein, E., Brozovsky, P., Wirt, R., & James, L. (1990). The efficacy of social-influence prevention programs versus "standard care": Are new initiatives needed? *Journal of Behavioral Medicine, 13,* 281-296.

Asher, S. R., & Coie, J. D. (Eds.). (1990). *Peer rejection in childhood.* New York: Cambridge University Press.

Bangert-Drowns, R. L. (1988). The effects of school-based substance abuse education: A meta-analysis. *Journal of Drug Education, 18,* 243-264.

Barnett, W. S. (1990). Benefits of compensatory preschool education. *Journal of Human Resources, 27,* 279-312.

Best, J. A. (1989). Intervention perspectives on school health promotion research. *Health Education Quarterly, 16,* 299-306.

Bosworth, K., & Cueto, S. (1994). Drug abuse prevention curricula in public and private schools in Indiana. *Journal of Drug Education, 24,* 21-31.

Bosworth, K., & Sailes, J. (1993). Content and teaching strategies in 10 selected drug abuse prevention curricula. *Journal of School Health, 63,* 247-253.

Botvin, G. J., Baker, E., Dusenbury, L., Botvin, E. M., & Diaz, T. (1995). Long-term follow-up results of a randomized drug abuse prevention trial in a white middle-class population. *Journal of the American Medical Association, 273,* 1106-1112.

Botvin, G. J., Schinke, S. P., Epstein, J. A., & Diaz, T. (1994). Effectiveness of culturally focused and generic skills training approaches to alcohol and drug abuse prevention among minority youth. *Psychology of Addictive Behaviors, 8,* 116-127.

Brooks-Gunn, J., McCormick, M. C., Shapiro, S., Benasich, A. A., & Black, G. W. (1994). The effects of early education intervention on maternal employment, public assistance, and health insurance: The Infant Health and Development Program. *American Journal of Public Health, 84,* 924-931.

Brooks-Gunn, J., & Paikoff, R. L. (1993). Sex is a gamble, kissing is a game: Adolescent sexuality and health promotion. In S. P. Millstein, A. Petersen, & E. Nightingale (Eds.), *Promotion of health behavior in adolescence* (pp. 180-208). New York: Carnegie Corporation.

Brophy, J. (1986). Teacher influences on student achievement. *American Psychologist, 41,* 1069-1077.

Bruvold, W. H. (1993). A meta-analysis of adolescent smoking prevention programs. *American Journal of Public Health, 83,* 872-880.

Buckner, J. C., Trickett, E. J., & Corse, S. J. (Eds.). (1985). *Primary prevention in mental health: An annotated bibliography* (DHHS Publication No. ADM 85-1405). Washington, DC: Government Printing Office.

Bush, P. J., Zuckerman, A. E., Theiss, P. K., Taggart, V. S., Horowitz, C., Sheridan, M. J., & Walter, H. J. (1989). Cardiovascular risk factor prevention in black schoolchildren: Two-year results of the "Know Your Body" program. *American Journal of Epidemiology, 129,* 466-482.

Cairns, R. B., Cairns, B. D., & Neckerman, H. J. (1989). Early school dropout: Configurations and determinants. *Child Development, 60,* 1437-1452.

Camp, B. W., Blom, G. E., Herbert, F., & Van Doorninck, W. J. (1977). "Think Aloud": A program for developing self-control in young aggressive boys. *Journal of Abnormal Child Psychology, 5,* 157-169.

Casto, G., & White, K. (1985). The efficacy of early intervention programs with environmentally at-risk infants. *Prevention in Human Services, 3,* 37-50.

Clarizio, H. F. (1979). School psychologists and the mental health needs of children. In G. D. Phye & D. J. Reschly (Eds.), *School psychology: Perspectives and issues* (pp. 181-216). New York: Academic Press.

Coates, T. J., Barofsky, I., Saylor, K. E., Simons-Morton, B., Huster, W., Sereghy, E., Straugh, S., Jacobs, H., & Kidd, L. (1985). Modifying the snack food consumption patterns of inner city high school students: The Great Sensations Study. *Preventive Medicine, 14,* 234-247.

Coben, J. H., Weiss, H. B., Mulvey, E. P., & Dearwater, S. R. (1994). A primer on school violence prevention. *Journal of School Health, 64,* 309-313.

Cohen, P. A., Kulik, J. A., & Kulik, C. C. (1982). Educational outcomes of tutoring: A meta-analysis of findings. *American Educational Research Journal, 19,* 237-248.

Coie, J. D., & Krehbiel, G. (1984). Effects of academic tutoring on the social status of low-achieving, socially rejected children. *Child Development, 55,* 1465-1478.

Coie, J. D., Watt, N. F., West, S. G., Hawkins, J. D., Asarnow, J. R., Markman, H. J., Ramey, S. L., Shure, M. B., & Long, B. (1993). The science of prevention: A conceptual framework and some directions for a national research program. *American Psychologist, 48,* 1013-1022.

Comer, J. P. (1985). The Yale-New Haven Primary Prevention Project: A follow-up study. *Journal of the American Academy of Child and Adolescent Psychiatry, 24,* 154-160.

Conduct Problems Prevention Research Group. (1992). A developmental and clinical model for the prevention of conduct disorder: The FAST Track Program. *Development and Psychopathology, 4,* 509-527.

Connell, D. B., Turner, R. R., & Mason, E. F. (1985). Summary of findings of the school health education evaluation: Health promotion effectiveness, implementation, and costs. *Journal of School Health, 55,* 316-321.

Cortese, P. A. (1993). Accomplishments in comprehensive school health education. *Journal of School Health, 63,* 21-23.

Cowen, E. L. (1980). The Primary Mental Health Project: Yesterday, today, and tomorrow. *Journal of Special Education, 14,* 134-154.

Cowen, E. L. (1986). Primary prevention in mental health: Ten years of retrospect and ten years of prospect. In M. Kessler & S. E. Goldston (Eds.), *A decade of progress in primary prevention* (pp. 3-45). Hanover, NH: University Press of New England.

Cowen, E. L., Dorr, D., Clarfield, S. P., Kreling, B., McWilliams, S. A., Pokracki, F., Pratt, D. M., Terrell, D. L., & Wilson, A. B. (1973). The AML: A quick screening device for early identification of school maladaptation. *American Journal of Community Psychology, 1,* 12-35.

Cowen, E. L., Hightower, D., Johnson, D. B., Sarno, M., & Weissberg, R. P. (1989). State-level dissemination of a program for early detection and prevention of school maladjustment. *Professional Psychology: Research and Practice, 20,* 309-314.

Cowen, E. L., Hightower, D., Pedro-Carroll, J., & Work, W. C. (1990). School-based models for primary prevention programming with children. In R. P. Lorion (Ed.), *Protecting the children: Strategies for optimizing emotional and behavioral development* (pp. 133-160). Binghampton, NY: Haworth.

Crockett, S. J., Mullis, R., Perry, C. L., & Luepker, R. V. (1989). Parent education in youth-directed nutrition interventions. *Preventive Medicine, 18,* 475-491.

DeCharms, R. (1972). Personal causation training in the schools. *Journal of Applied Social Psychology, 2,* 95-113.

Dielman, T. E. (1994). School-based research on the prevention of adolescent alcohol use and misuse: Methodological issues and advances. *Journal of Research on Adolescence, 4,* 271-293.

Dielman, T. E., Shope, J. T., Leech, S. L., & Butchart, A. T. (1989). Differential effectiveness of an elementary school-based alcohol misuse prevention program. *Journal of School Health, 59,* 255-263.

Digiuseppe, R., & Kassinove, H. (1976). Effects of a rational-emotive school mental health program on children's emotional adjustment. *Journal of Community Psychology, 4,* 382-387.

Dryfoos, J. G. (1990). *Adolescents at risk: Prevalence and prevention.* New York: Oxford University Press.

Dumas, J. E. (1989). Treating antisocial behavior in children: Child and family approaches. *Clinical Psychology Review, 9,* 197-222.

Durlak, J. A. (1977). Description and evaluation of a behaviorally oriented school-based preventive mental health program. *Journal of Consulting and Clinical Psychology, 45,* 27-33.

Durlak, J. A. (1983). Providing mental health services to elementary school children. In C. E. Walker & M. C. Roberts (Eds.), *Handbook of clinical child psychology* (pp. 660-679). New York: John Wiley.

Durlak, J. A. (1994). Understanding meta analysis. In L. Grimm & P. Yarnold (Eds.), *Reading and understanding multivariate statistics* (pp. 319-352). Washington, DC: American Psychological Association.

Durlak, J. A., & Jason, L. A. (1984). Preventive programs for school-aged children and adolescents. In M. C. Roberts & L. Peterson (Eds.), *Prevention of problems in childhood: Psychological research and applications* (pp. 103-132). New York: John Wiley.

Durlak, J. A., Lampman, C., Wells, A., & Cotten, J. (1993, June). A review of primary prevention programs for children and adolescents. In J. A. Durlak (Chair), *Evaluation of primary prevention: Programs, outcomes, and issues.* Symposium conducted at the Fourth Biennial Conference on Community Research and Action, Williamsburg, VA.

Durlak, J. A., & Lipsey, M. W. (1991). A practitioner's guide to meta-analysis. *American Journal of Community Psychology, 19,* 291-332.

Durlak, J. A., & Wells, A. M. (1994, October). *An evaluation of secondary prevention mental health programs for children and adolescents.* Paper presented at the First Annual Kansas Conference on Child Clinical Psychology, Lawrence, KS.

Dusenbury, L., Botvin, G. J., & James-Ortiz, S. (1990). The primary prevention of adolescent substance abuse through the promotion of personal and social competence. In R. P. Lorion (Ed.), *Protecting the children: Strategies for optimizing emotional and behavioral development* (pp. 201-224). Binghamton, NY: Haworth.

Elder, J. P., Wildey, M., de Moor, C., Sallis, J. F., Jr., Eckhardt, L., Edwards, C., Erickson, A., Golbeck, A., Hovell, M., Johnson, D., Levitz, M. D., Molgaard, C., Young, R., Vito, D., & Woodruff, S. I. (1993). The long-term prevention of tobacco use among junior high school students: Classroom and telephone interventions. *American Journal of Public Health, 83,* 1239-1244.

Ellison, R. C., Capper, A. L., Goldberg, R. J., Witschi, J. C., & Stare, F. J. (1989). The environmental component: Changing school food service to promote cardiovascular health. *Health Education Quarterly, 16,* 285-297.

Emery, R. E. (1988). *Marriage, divorce, and children's adjustment.* Newbury Park, CA: Sage.

Ennett, S. T., Tobler, N. S., Ringwalt, C. L., & Flewelling, R. L. (1994). How effective is drug abuse resistance education? A meta-analysis of Project DARE outcome evaluations. *American Journal of Public Health, 84,* 1394-1401.

Ensminger, M. E., & Slusarick, A. L. (1992). Paths to high school graduation or dropout: A longitudinal study of a first-grade cohort. *Sociology of Education, 65,* 95-113.

Errecart, M. T., Walberg, H. J., Ross, J. G., Gold, R. S., Fiedler, J. L., & Kolbe, L. J. (1991). Effectiveness of Teenage Health Teaching Modules. *Journal of School Health, 61,* 26-30.

Evertson, C. M. (1985). Training teachers in classroom management: An experiment in secondary school classrooms. *Journal of Educational Research, 79,* 51-58.

Evertson, C. M., Emmer, E. T., Sanford, J. P., & Clements, B. S. (1983). Improving classroom management: An experiment in elementary school classrooms. *Elementary School Journal, 84,* 173-188.

Felner, R. D., & Adan, A. M. (1988). The School Transition Environment Project: An ecological intervention and evaluation. In R. H. Price, E. L. Cowen, R. P. Lorion, & J. Ramos-McKay (Eds.), *14 ounces of prevention: A casebook for practitioners* (pp. 111-122). Washington, DC: American Psychological Association.

Felner, R. D., Brand, S., Adan, A. M., Mulhall, P. F., Flowers, N., Sartain, B., & DuBois, D. L. (1993). Restructuring the ecology of the school as an approach to prevention during school transitions: Longitudinal follow-ups and extensions of the School Transitional Environment Project (STEP). *Prevention in Human Services, 10,* 103-136.

Flannery, D. J., & Torquati, J. (1993). An elementary school substance abuse prevention program: Teacher and administrator perspectives. *Journal of Drug Education, 23,* 387-397.

Flay, B. R. (1985). Psychosocial approaches to smoking prevention: A review of findings. *Health Psychology, 4,* 449-488.

Flay, B. R. (1986). Efficacy and effectiveness trials (and other phases of research) in the development of health promotion programs. *Preventive Medicine, 15,* 451-474.

Flynn, B. S., Worden, J. K., Secker-Walker, R. H., Pirie, P. L., Badger, G. J., Carpenter, J. H., & Geller, B. M. (1994). Mass media and school interventions for cigarette smoking prevention: Effects 2 years after completion. *American Journal of Public Health, 84,* 1148-1150.

Fredericksen, L. W., Solomon, L. J., & Brehony, K. A. (Eds.). (1984). *Marketing health behavior: Principles, techniques and applications.* New York: Plenum.

Fullan, M. G. (1991). *The new meaning of educational change* (2nd ed.). New York: Teachers College Press.

Fullan, M. G. (1992). *Successful school improvement: The implementation perspective and beyond.* Philadelphia: Open University Press.

Furstenberg, F. F., Jr., Brooks-Gunn, J., & Morgan, S. P. (1987). *Adolescent mothers in later life.* Cambridge, UK: Cambridge University Press.

Gettinger, M. (1988). Methods of proactive classroom management. *School Psychology Review, 17,* 227-242.

Gingiss, P. L., Gottlieb, N. H., & Brink, S. G. (1994). Increasing teacher receptivity toward use of tobacco prevention education programs. *Journal of Drug Education, 24,* 163-176.

Glidewell, J. G., Gildea, M. C. L., & Kaufman, M. K. (1973). The preventive and therapeutic effects of two school mental health programs. *American Journal of Community Psychology, 1,* 295-329.

Glidewell, J. G., & Swallow, C. S. (1969). *The prevalence of maladjustment in elementary schools* (Report prepared for the Joint Commission on Mental Health of Children). Chicago: University of Chicago Press.

Good, T. L., & Weinstein, R. S. (1986). Schools make a difference: Evidence, criticisms, and new directions. *American Psychologist, 41,* 1090-1097.

Goodlad, J. I. (1991). Why we need a complete redesign of teacher education. *Educational Leadership, 49,* 4-6.

Gottfredson, D. C. (1987). An evaluation of an organization development approach to reducing school disorder. *Evaluation Review, 11,* 739-763.

Greenwood, C. R., Delquadri, J. C., & Hall, R. V. (1989). Longitudinal effects of classwide peer tutoring. *Journal of Educational Psychology, 81,* 371-383.

Grych, J. H., & Fincham, F. D. (1992). Interventions for children of divorce: Toward greater integration of research and action. *Psychological Bulletin, 111,* 434-454.

Gullotta, T. P. (1994). The what, who, why, where, when, and how of primary prevention. *Journal of Primary Prevention, 15,* 5-14.

Hansen, W. B. (1992). School-based substance abuse prevention: A review of the state of the art in curriculum, 1980-1990. *Health Education Research, 7,* 403-430.

Hansen, W. B., & Graham, J. W. (1991). Preventing alcohol, marijuana, and cigarette use among adolescents: Peer pressure resistance training versus establishing conservative norms. *Preventive Medicine, 20,* 414-430.

Hartman, L. M. (1979). The preventive reduction of psychological risk in asymptomatic adolescents. *American Journal of Orthopsychiatry, 49,* 121-135.

Hawkins, J. D., Catalano, R. F., & Miller, J. Y. (1992). Risk and protective factors for alcohol and other drug problems in adolescence and early adulthood: Implications for substance abuse prevention. *Psychological Bulletin, 112,* 64-105.

Hawkins, J. D., Von Cleve, E., & Catalano, R. F., Jr. (1991). Reducing early childhood aggression: Results of a primary prevention program. *Journal of the American Academy of Child and Adolescent Psychiatry, 30,* 208-217.

Heller, K., Price, R. H., & Sher, K. J. (1980). Research and evaluation in primary prevention: Issues and guidelines. In R. H. Price, R. F. Ketterer, B. C. Bader, & J. Monahan (Eds.), *Prevention in mental health: Research, policy, and practice* (pp. 285-313). Beverly Hills, CA: Sage.

Holtzman, D., Greene, B. Z., Ingraham, G. C., Daily, L. A., Demchuk, D. G., & Kolbe, L. J. (1992). HIV education and health education in the United States: A national survey of local school district policies and practices. *Journal of School Health, 62,* 421-427.

Horacek, H. J., Ramey, C. T., Campbell, F. A., Hoffmann, K. P., & Fletcher, R. H. (1987). Predicting school failure and assessing early intervention with high-risk children. *Journal of the American Academy of Child and Adolescent Psychiatry, 26,* 758-763.

House, E. R. (1974). *The politics of educational innovation.* Berkeley, CA: McCutchan.

Huberman, A. M., & Miles, M. B. (1984). *Innovation up close.* New York: Plenum.

Institute of Medicine. (1994). *Reducing risks for mental disorders: Frontiers for preventive intervention research.* Washington, DC: National Academy Press.

Jansen, M. A., & Johnson, E. M. (Eds.). (1993). Methodological issues in prevention research [Special Issue]. *American Journal of Community Psychology, 21*(5).

Jason, L. A., & Bogat, G. A. (1983). Preventive behavioral interventions. In R. D. Felner, L. A. Jason, J. N. Moritsugu, & S. S. Farber (Eds.), *Preventive psychology: Theory, research and practice* (pp. 128-148). Elmsford, NY: Pergamon.

Jason, L. A., Thompson, D., & Rose, T. (1986). Methodological issues in prevention. In B. A. Edelstein & L. Michelson (Eds.), *Handbook of prevention* (pp. 1-19). New York: Plenum.

Jason, L. A., Weine, A. M., Johnson, J. H., Warren-Sohlberg, L., Filippelli, L. A., Turner, E. Y., & Lardon, C. (1992). *Helping transfer students: Strategies for educational and social readjustment.* San Francisco: Jossey-Bass.

Jemmott, J. B., III, Jemmott, L. S., & Fong, G. T. (1992). Reductions in HIV risk-associated sexual behaviors among black male adolescents: Effects of an AIDS prevention intervention. *American Journal of Public Health, 82,* 372-377.

Johnson, C. A., Pentz, M. A., Weber, M. D., Dwyer, J. H., Baer, N., MacKinnon, D. P., Hansen, W. B., & Flay, B. R. (1990). Relative effectiveness of comprehensive community programming for drug abuse prevention with high-risk and low-risk adolescents. *Journal of Consulting and Clinical Psychology, 58,* 447-456.

Johnson, D. L. (1988). Primary prevention of behavior problems in young children: The Houston Parent-Child Development Center. In R. H. Price, E. L. Cowen, R. P. Lorion, & J. Ramos-McKay (Eds.), *14 ounces of prevention: A casebook for practitioners* (pp. 44-52). Washington, DC: American Psychological Association.

Johnston, L. D., O'Malley, P. M., & Bachman, J. G. (1986). *Drug use among American high school schools, college students and other young adults: National trends through 1985.* Rockville, MD: National Institute on Drug Abuse.

Kahn, J. S., Kehle, T. J., Jenson, W. R., & Clark, E. (1990). Comparison of cognitive-behavioral, relaxation, and self-modeling interventions for depression among middle-school students. *School Psychology Review, 19,* 196-211.

Kaplan, R. M. (1984). The connection between clinical health promotion and health status. *American Psychologist, 39,* 755-765.

Kaufman, J. S., Jason, L. A., Sawlski, L. M., & Halpert, J. A. (1994). A comprehensive multi-media program to prevent smoking among black students. *Journal of Drug Education, 24,* 95-108.

Kazdin, A. E. (1987). *Conduct disorder in childhood and adolescence.* Newbury Park, CA: Sage.

Kazdin, A. E. (1990). Psychotherapy for children and adolescents. *Annual Review of Psychology, 41,* 21-54.

Kazdin, A. E., Bass, D., Ayers, W. A., & Rodgers, A. (1990). Empirical and clinical focus of child and adolescent psychotherapy research. *Journal of Consulting and Clinical Psychology, 58,* 729-740.

Kellam, S. G., Rebok, G. W., Ialongo, N., & Mayer, L. S. (1994). The course and malleability of aggressive behavior from early first grade into middle school: Results of a developmental epidemiologically-based preventive trial. *Journal of Child Psychology and Psychiatry, 35,* 259-281.

Kelly, J. G. (1988). *A guide to conducting prevention research in the community: First steps.* Binghampton, NY: Haworth.

Kirby, D., Short, L., Collins, J., Rugg, D., Kolbe, L., Howard, L., Miller, B., Sonenstein, F., & Zabin, L. S. (1994). School-based programs to reduce sexual risk behaviors: A review of effectiveness. *Public Health Reports, 109,* 339-360.

Kirschenbaum, D. S., DeVoge, J. B., Marsh, M. E., & Steffen, J. J. (1980). Multimodal evaluation of therapy vs. consultation components in a large inner-city early intervention program. *American Journal of Community Psychology, 8,* 587-601.

Klein, S. S. (1993). Sharing the best: Finding better ways for the federal government to use evaluation to guide the dissemination of promising and exemplary education solutions. *Evaluation and Program Planning, 16,* 213-217.

Knitzer, J., Steinberg, Z., & Fleisch, B. (1990). *At the schoolhouse door: An examination of programs and policies for children with behavioral and emotional problems.* New York: Bank Street College of Education.

La Greca, A. M., & Santogrossi, D. A. (1980). Social skills training with elementary school students: A behavioral group approach. *Journal of Consulting and Clinical Psychology, 48,* 220-227.

Lamb, H. R., & Zusman, J. (1979). Primary prevention in perspective. *American Journal of Psychiatry, 136,* 12-17.

Lavin, A. T. (1993). Comprehensive school health education: Barriers and opportunities. *Journal of School Health, 63,* 24-27.

Lazar, I., & Darlington, R. (1982). Lasting effects of early education: A report from the Consortium for Longitudinal Studies. *Monographs of the Society for Research in Child Development, 47*(2-3, Serial No. 195).

Light, R. J., & Pillemer, D. B. (1984). *Summing up: The science of reviewing research.* Cambridge, MA: Harvard University Press.

Lipsey, M. W., & Wilson, D. B. (1993). The efficacy of psychological, educational, and behavioral treatment. *American Psychologist, 48,* 1181-1209.

Lochman, J. E., Burch, P. R., Curry, J. F., & Lampron, L. B. (1984). Treatment and generalization effects of cognitive-behavioral and goal-setting interventions with aggressive boys. *Journal of Consulting and Clinical Psychology, 52,* 915-916.

Lochman, J. E., Coie, J. D., Underwood, M. K., & Terry, R. (1993). Effectiveness of a social relations intervention program for aggressive and nonaggressive, rejected children. *Journal of Consulting and Clinical Psychology, 61,* 1053-1058.

Loeber, R. (1990). Development and risk factors of juvenile antisocial behavior and delinquency. *Clinical Psychology Review, 10,* 1-41.

Long, B. B. (1989). The Mental Health Association and prevention: A history. In R. C. Hess & J. DeLeon (Eds.), *The National Mental Health Association: Eighty years of involvement in the field of prevention* (pp. 5-44). Binghamton, NY: Haworth.

Lorion, R. P. (1990). Evaluating HIV risk-reduction efforts: Ten lessons from psychotherapy and prevention outcome strategies. *Journal of Community Psychology, 18,* 325-336.

Males, M. (1993). School-age pregnancy: Why hasn't prevention worked? *Journal of School Health, 63,* 429-432.

McGrew, J. H., Bond, G. R., Dieten, L., & Salyers, M. (1994). Measuring the fidelity of implementation of a mental health program model. *Journal of Consulting and Clinical Psychology, 62,* 670-678.

McKinlay, S. M., Stone, E. J., & Zucker, D. M. (1989). Research design and analysis issues. *Health Education Quarterly, 16,* 307-313.

McMahon, R. J. (1994). Diagnosis, assessment, and treatment of externalizing problems in children: The role of longitudinal data. *Journal of Consulting and Clinical Psychology, 62,* 901-917.

Meisels, S. J., & Liaw, F. R. (1993). Failure in grade: Do retained students catch up? *Journal of Educational Research, 87,* 69-77.

Miller, B. C., Card, J. J., Paikoff, R. L., & Peterson, J. L. (Eds.). (1992). *Preventing adolescent pregnancy: Model programs and evaluations.* Newbury Park, CA: Sage.

Montagne, M., & Scott, D. M. (1993). Prevention of substance use problems: Models, factors, and processes. *International Journal of the Addictions, 28,* 1177-1208.

Moos, R. H. (1979). *Evaluating educational environments.* San Francisco: Jossey-Bass.

Murphy, J. (Ed.). (1990). *The educational reform movement of the 1980s.* Berkeley, CA: McCutchan.

National Center for Education Statistics. (1986). *Annual digest of education statistics.* Washington, DC: U.S. Department of Education, Office of Educational Research Improvement.

National Commission on Children. (1991). *Beyond rhetoric: A new American agenda for children and families.* Washington, DC: Government Printing Office.

Oden, S., & Asher, S. R. (1977). Coaching children in social skills for friendship making. *Child Development, 48,* 495-506.

O'Donnell, J., Hawkins, J. D., Catalano, R. F., Abbott, R. D., & Day, L. E. (1995). Preventing school failure, drug use, and delinquency among low-income children: Effects of a long-term prevention project in elementary schools. *American Journal of Orthopsychiatry, 65,* 87-100.

Olweus, D. (1993). *Bullying at school: What we know and what we can do.* Oxford, UK: Basil Blackwell.

Parcel, G. S., Simons-Morton, B., O'Hara, N. M., Baranowski, T., & Wilson, B. (1989). School promotion of healthful diet and physical activity: Impact on learning outcomes and self-reported behavior. *Health Education Quarterly, 16,* 181-199.

Pentz, M. A. (1986). Community organization and school liaisons: How to get programs started. *Journal of School Health, 56,* 382-388.

Perry, C. L. (1984). Health promotion at school: Expanding the potential for prevention. *School Psychology Review, 13,* 141-149.

Perry, C. L., Crockett, S. J., & Pirie, P. (1987). Influencing parental health behavior: Implications of community assessments. *Health Education, 18,* 68-77.

Perry, C. L., Luepker, R. V., Murray, D. M., Kurth, C., Mullis, R., Crockett, S., & Jacobs, D. R., Jr. (1988). Parent involvement with children's health promotion: The Minnesota Home Team. *American Journal of Public Health, 78,* 1156-1160.

Price, R. H. (1986). Education for prevention. In M. Kessler & S. E. Goldston (Eds.), *A decade of progress in primary prevention* (pp. 289-306). Hanover, NH: University Press of New England.

Price, R. H., Cowen, E. L., Lorion, R. P., & Ramos-McKay, J. (1989). The search for effective prevention programs: What we learned along the way. *American Journal of Orthopsychiatry, 59,* 49-58.

Prinz, R. J., Blechman, E. A., & Dumas, J. E. (1994). An evaluation of peer coping-skills training for childhood aggression. *Journal of Clinical Child Psychology, 23,* 193-203.

Purkey, S. C., & Smith, M. S. (1983). Effective schools: A review. *Elementary School Journal, 83,* 427-452.

Resnicow, K., Cherry, J., & Cross, D. (1993). Ten unanswered questions regarding comprehensive school health promotion. *Journal of School Health, 63,* 171-175.

Resnicow, K., Cohn, L., Reinhardt, J., Cross, D., Futterman, R., Kirschner, E., Wynder, E. L., & Allegrante, J. P. (1992). A three-year evaluation of the Know Your Body program in inner-city schoolchildren. *Health Education Quarterly, 19,* 463-480.

Resnicow, K., Cross, D., & Wynder, E. L. (1991). The role of comprehensive school-based interventions: The results of four Know Your Body studies. *Annals of the New York Academy of Sciences, 623,* 285-298.

Rickel, A. U., & Allen, L. (1987). *Preventing maladjustment from infancy through adolescence.* Newbury Park, CA: Sage.

Rogers, E. M. (1983). *Diffusion of innovations* (3rd ed.). New York: Free Press.

Rohrbach, L. A., Graham, J. W., & Hansen, W. B. (1993). Diffusion of a school-based substance abuse prevention program: Predictors of program implementation. *Preventive Medicine, 22,* 237-260.

Rolf, J. E. (1985). Evolving adaptive theories and methods for prevention research with children. *Journal of Consulting and Clinical Psychology, 53,* 631-646.

Rosenthal, R., & Rubin, D. B. (1982). A simple, general purpose display of magnitude of experimental effect. *Journal of Educational Psychology, 74,* 166-169.

Ross, J. G., Luepker, R. V., Nelson, G. D., Saavedra, P., & Hubbard, B. M. (1991). Teenage Health Teaching Modules: Impact of teacher training on implementation and student outcomes. *Journal of School Health, 61,* 31-34.

Rowan, B., & Guthrie, L. F. (1989). The quality of Chapter 1 instruction: Results from a study of twenty-four schools. In R. E. Slavin, N. L. Karweit, & N. A. Madden (Eds.), *Effective programs for students at risk* (pp. 195-219). Needham Heights, MA: Allyn & Bacon.

Rutter, M. (1979). Protective factors in children's responses to stress and disadvantage. In M. Whalen & J. E. Rolf (Eds.), *Primary prevention of psychopathology: Vol. 3. Social competence in children* (pp. 49-74). Hanover, NH: University Press of New England.

Rutter, M. (1983). School effects on pupil progress: Research findings and policy implications. *Child Development, 54,* 1-29.

Rutter, M. (1994). Beyond longitudinal data: Causes, consequences, changes, and continuity. *Journal of Consulting and Clinical Psychology, 62,* 928-940.

Sallis, J. F., Simons-Morton, B. G., Stone, E. J., Corbin, C. B., Epstein, L. H., Faucette, N., Klesges, R. C., Petray, C. K., Rowland, T. W., & Taylor, W. C. (1992). Determinants of physical activity and interventions in youth. *Medicine and Science in Sports and Exercise, 24*(Suppl.), S248-S257.

Sarason, S. B. (1971). *The culture of the school and the problem of change.* Boston: Allyn & Bacon.

Sarason, S. B. (1990). *The predictable failure of educational reform: Can we change course before it's too late?* San Francisco: Jossey-Bass.

Sarason, S. B. (1993). *The case for change: Rethinking the preparation of educators.* San Francisco: Jossey-Bass.

Scanlon, J. W., Horst, P., Nay, J. N., Schmidt, R. E., & Waller, A. E. (1977). Evaluability assessment: Avoiding Type III and IV errors. In G. R. Gilbert & P. J. Conklin (Eds.), *Evaluation management: A source book of readings* (pp. 71-90). Charlottesville, VA: U.S. Civil Service Commission.

Scheirer, M. A. (1990). The life cycle of an innovation: Adoption versus discontinuation of the fluoride mouth rinse program in schools. *Journal of Health and Social Behavior, 31,* 203-215.

Schinke, S. P. (1994). Prevention science and practice: An agenda for action. *Journal of Primary Prevention, 15,* 45-57.

Schinke, S. P., Botvin, G. J., & Orlandi, M. A. (1991). *Substance abuse in children and adolescents: Evaluation and intervention.* Newbury Park, CA: Sage.

Schweinhart, L. J., & Weikart, D. B. (1988). The High/Scope Perry Preschool Program. In R. H. Price, E. L. Cowen, R. P. Lorion, & J. Ramos-McKay (Eds.), *14 ounces of prevention: A casebook for practitioners* (pp. 53-65). Washington, DC: American Psychological Association.

Sechrest, L. B. (1993). Preventing problems in prevention research. *American Journal of Community Psychology, 21,* 665-679.

Slavin, R. E., Karweit, N. L., & Madden, N. A. (Ed.). (1989). *Effective programs for students at risk.* Needham Heights, MA: Allyn & Bacon.

Slavin, R. E., Karweit, N. L., & Wasik, B. A. (1994). *Preventing early school failure.* Needham Heights, MA: Allyn & Bacon.

Smith, D. W., McCormick, L. K., Steckler, A. B., & McLeroy, K. R. (1993). Teachers' use of health curricula: Implementation of Growing Healthy, Project SMART, and the Teenage Health Teaching Modules. *Journal of School Health, 63,* 349-354.

Spivack, G., & Shure, M. (1974). *Social adjustment of young children: A cognitive approach to solving real-life problems.* San Francisco: Jossey-Bass.

Stark, K. D., Reynolds, W. M., & Kaslow, N. J. (1987). A comparison of the relative efficacy of self-control therapy and a behavioral problem-solving therapy for depression in children. *Journal of Abnormal Child Psychology, 15,* 91-113.

Stolz, S. B. (1981). Adoption of innovation from applied behavioral research: "Does anybody care?" *Journal of Applied Behavior Analysis, 14,* 491-505.

Taggart, V. S., Bush, P. J., Zuckerman, A. E., & Theiss, P. K. (1990). A process evaluation of the District of Columbia "Know Your Body" project. *Journal of School Health, 60,* 60-66.

Tobler, N. S. (1986). Meta-analysis of 143 adolescent drug prevention programs: Quantitative outcome results of program participants compared to a control or comparison group. *Journal of Drug Issues, 16,* 537-567.

Toro, P. A., Cowen, E. L., Gesten, E. L., Weissberg, R. P., Rapkin, B. D., & Davidson, E. (1985). Social environmental predictors of children's adjustment in elementary school classrooms. *American Journal of Community Psychology, 13,* 353-364.

Tremblay, R. E., Vitaro, F., Bertrand, L., LeBlanc, M., Beauchesne, H., Boileau, H., & David, L. (1992). Parent and child training to prevent early onset of delinquency: The Montreal Longitudinal-Experimental Study. In J. McCord & R. E. Tremblay (Eds.), *Preventing antisocial behavior: Interventions from birth through adolescence* (pp. 117-137). New York: Guilford.

U.S. Department of Health and Human Services. (1989). *Healthy people 2000: National health promotion and disease prevention objectives* (Publication No. PHS 91-50212). Washington, DC: Government Printing Office.

Walter, H. J., & Vaughan, R. D. (1993). AIDS risk reduction among a multiethnic sample of urban high school students. *Journal of the American Medical Association, 270,* 725-730.

Weinstein, R. S., Soule, C. R., Collins, R., Cone, J., Mehlhorn, M., & Simontacchi, K. (1991). Expectations and high school change: Teacher-researcher collaboration to prevent school failure. *American Journal of Community Psychology, 19,* 333-363.

Weissberg, R. P., Caplan, M. Z., & Harwood, R. L. (1991). Promoting competent young people in competence-enhancing environments: A systems-based perspective on primary prevention. *Journal of Consulting and Clinical Psychology, 59,* 830-841.

Weissberg, R. P., Caplan, M. Z., & Sivo, P. J. (1989). A new conceptual framework for establishing school-based social competence promotion programs. In L. A. Bond & B. E. Compas (Eds.), *Primary prevention and promotion in the schools* (pp. 255-296). Newbury Park, CA: Sage.

White, C. P., & White, M. B. (1991). The Adolescent Family Life Act: Content, findings, and policy recommendations for pregnancy prevention programs. *Journal of Clinical Child Psychology, 20,* 58-70.

White, J. L., Moffitt, T. E., Earls, F., Robins, L., & Silva, P. A. (1990). How early can we tell? Predictors of childhood conduct disorder and adolescent delinquency. *Criminology, 28,* 507-528.

Wilson, N. H., & Rotter, J. C. (1986). Anxiety management training and study skills counseling for students on self-esteem and test anxiety and performance. *School Counselor, 34,* 18-31.

Yoshikawa, H. (1994). Prevention as cumulative protection: Effects of early family support and education on chronic delinquency and its risks. *Psychological Bulletin, 115,* 28-54.

Zabin, L. S., Hirsch, M. B., Street, R., Emerson, M. R., Hardy, J. B., & King, T. M. (1986). The Baltimore Pregnancy Prevention Program for urban teenagers: I. How did it work? *Family Planning Perspectives, 20,* 182-187.

NAME INDEX

SUBJECT INDEX

ABOUT THE AUTHOR

Joseph A. Durlak is Professor of Psychology at Loyola University, Chicago. He received his Ph.D. from Vanderbilt University in 1972 and then served in the U.S. Army as a clinical psychologist and began his work on school-based prevention programs. He joined the psychology faculty at Southern Illinois University in Carbondale in 1976 and then moved to Loyola in 1980. During his tenure at Loyola he has directed the doctoral clinical psychology training program. He is a fellow of the American Psychological Association and is on the editorial boards of the *American Journal of Community Psychology, Journal of Community Psychology, Death Studies,* and *Omega: Journal of Death and Dying.* His major research interests are in the areas of community psychology and child clinical psychology, particularly with respect to prevention and the use of paraprofessionals.